The Hours of the Universe

Other Orbis books from Ilia Delio

Christ in Evolution

The Emergent Christ:
Exploring the Meaning of Catholic in an
Evolutionary Universe

The Unbearable Wholeness of Being:
God, Evolution, and the Power of Love

From Teilhard to Omega:
Co-Creating an Unfinished Universe

Making All Things New:
Catholicity, Cosmology, Consciousness

Birth of a Dancing Star:
My Journey from Cradle Catholic to Cyborg Christian

Re-Enchanting the Earth:
Why AI Needs Religion

The Hours of the Universe

Reflections on God, Science, and the Human Journey

Ilia Delio, OSF

ORBIS BOOKS
Maryknoll, New York 10545

Founded in 1970, Orbis Books endeavors to publish works that enlighten the mind, nourish the spirit, and challenge the conscience. The publishing arm of the Maryknoll Fathers and Brothers, Orbis seeks to explore the global dimensions of the Christian faith and mission, to invite dialogue with diverse cultures and religious traditions, and to serve the cause of reconciliation and peace. The books published reflect the views of their authors and do not represent the official position of the Maryknoll Society. To learn more about Maryknoll and Orbis Books, please visit our website at www.orbisbooks.com.

Copyright © 2021 by Ilia Delio, OSF

Published by Orbis Books, Box 302, Maryknoll, NY 10545-0302.

All rights reserved.

No part of this publication may be reproduced or transmitted in any form or by any means, electronic or mechanical, including photocopying, recording, or any information storage or retrieval system, without prior permission in writing from the publisher.

Thanks to the Global Sisters Report for permission to reprint the following pieces that originally appeared on their blog: "Living in a Wavy Universe" (March 7, 2016); "Quantum Edge Catholicity" (November 15, 2016); "Mercy and the Humility of God" (January 7, 2016); "God in the Midst of Pain" (July 25, 2016); "Lex Credendi, Lex Vivendi: A Response to *Laudato Si'*" (June 30, 2015); "Can a Renewal of Inner Space Help Heal the Earth?" (April 18, 2017); "Beatrice Bruteau, Pope Francis, and Global Community" (September 27, 2015); "Can Consumer People Be Christmas People?" (December 29, 2016); "Radical Forgiveness: Lessons from Nature" (March 30, 2015); "Time to Become Ultrahuman?" (January 9, 2018); "What Would Teilhard Say? Evolve or Be Annihilated?" (June 27, 2017); "Brother Mango and Eternal Life" (February 9, 2015).

Queries regarding rights and permissions should be addressed to Orbis Books, P.O. Box 302, Maryknoll, NY 10545-0302.

Manufactured in the United States of America
Manuscript editing and typesetting by Joan Weber Laflamme

Library of Congress Cataloging-in-Publication Data

Names: Delio, Ilia, author.
Title: The hours of the universe / Ilia Delio, OSF.
Description: Maryknoll, NY : Orbis Books, [2021] | Includes bibliographical references and index. | Summary: Drawing on work of Pierre Teilhard de Chardin and modern science, author offers meditations pointing toward a new understanding of Christianity in terms of evolution
Identifiers: LCCN 2020031296 (print) | LCCN 2020031297 (ebook) | ISBN 9781626984035 (rint) | ISBN 9781608338672 (ebook)
Subjects: LCSH: Evolution—Religious aspects—Christianity. | Religion and science. | Teilhard de Chardin, Pierre.
Classification: LCC BT712 .D45 2020 (print) | LCC BT712 (ebook) | DDC 261.5/5—dc23
LC record available at https://lccn.loc.gov/2020031296
LC ebook record available at https://lccn.loc.gov/2020031297

Contents

Acknowledgments   ix

Introduction   xi

Matins

1. Living in a Wavy Universe   3
2. Quantum Edge Catholicity   7
3. A Big Thinker for a Big Universe—
   Teilhard de Chardin   13

Lauds

4. Can We Discover God Anew?   21
5. Mercy and the Humility of God   27
6. God in the Midst of Pain   35
7. Do We Make a Difference to God?   39
8. One Eye, One Self, One God   45

Prime

9. Teilhard's Christian Pantheism   53
10. Lex Credendi, Lex Vivendi: *Laudato Si'*   57
11. Pope Francis and Saint Francis   69
12. Warming, Warming, Gone! Who Will Survive
    Climate Change?   77
13. Can a Renewal of Inner Space Help
    Heal the Earth?   87

14. Beatrice Bruteau, Pope Francis, and
    Global Community   93

Terce

15. The Cosmic Christ   103
16. Christ, the Future   107
17. The Rainbow of Pride   111
18. Race and Axial Consciousness   115

Sext

19. The Core Energy of Love   127
20. The Power of Faith   131
21. Fire Burns and So Does Love   135
22. The Ineffable Bond of Love   143

None

23. Despite the News, We Belong to One Another   149
24. Praying in Teilhard's Universe   155
25. Contemplation and Vision   163
26. Eucharist and God's Love   169
27. Teilhard's Troubled Worship   177
28. Can Consumer People Be Christmas People?   183
29. Internet Easter   189

Vespers

30. Radical Forgiveness—Lessons from Nature   199
31. Costly Love   205
32. Time to Become Ultrahuman?   211

Compline

33. Evolve or Be Annihilated   219

34. Hope in a Time of Crisis   227

35. Brother Mango and Eternal Life   235

Conclusion   239

Index   243

Acknowledgments

This book was brought to completion thanks to the valiant efforts of Gregory Hansell, executive director of the Christic Center, and Villanova doctoral students Jillian Langford and Robert Nicastro. Robert kindly read the original draft and provided very helpful feedback. I had planned to complete the book during the summer, but my plans were changed by a bicycle accident that left me with a concussion. Greg, Jillian, and Robert formed a team to finalize the footnotes and together helped bring this work to completion. It is to these young, committed theologians that I dedicate this book.

Introduction

In the brief span of the last two decades we have experienced a number of major crises, including the terrorist attacks of 9/11, protracted wars in the Middle East, the recession that followed the mortgage crisis of 2008, persistent racism, and more recently, the COVID-19 pandemic. Each crisis has brought about profound loss, and yet we manage to pick up the pieces and move on, as if these crises were merely interruptions in our otherwise normal lives. In a fragile world of finite limits, the breakdown of systems is not unusual. What is startling, however, is that within twenty short years, the number of human casualties due to catastrophic events has risen exponentially.

Profound suffering can evoke different responses. We may mourn our losses, especially the loss of loved ones to tragedy. But we may also recognize in these disruptions a call to awaken from our cultural stupor to the signs of a new reality breaking forth in our midst. We may long for what we have lost, but are we also able to read the signs of the times? Can we discern a new reality on the horizon?

The New Testament calls our attention to the in-breaking reign of God. The message of Jesus was one of seeing, believing, and trusting in the empowering presence of God. God is doing new things, Jesus proclaimed, but only those with new minds and hearts can see a new world breaking through the cracks of the old. Jesus offered a new set of values, teaching us how to live on the edge of a new tomorrow. We must make a choice, however, to embrace these new values and to live in a new way. The spiritual masters called this process of change "conversion": an unlearning of old habits that block the light of the new reality and a turning of the mind and heart in grace in order to entrust our lives to the living presence of God. Only if we believe in a new power in our midst can we let go of the old reins of control and allow the Spirit to draw us toward a new future.

We know the Christian message as a set of instructions, but do we know it as a new way of life? Its basic message is simple: God is doing new things through us; we are the new creation in process. Hence, the most unchristian position we can assume is to block the new creation from taking place. And that is exactly where the institutional church finds itself today, internally divided and defending itself against the cultural winds of change. The marginalization of religion from culture, the opposition of religion to evolution, and the reduction of religion to privatized forms of spirituality have left the world stripped of God, bereft of meaning and purpose. It is a world gone blind, turned inward, satiated with things, and unconscious of its fundamental interdependency. Nothing really binds us together, and we find ourselves in a world of fear and resistance. We are skeptical of any new reality because we fear that rearranging our lives will disrupt the comfortable niches we have come to inhabit. We have a condition of chronic low-level depression driven by fear and distrust. And yet there is also a deep dimension of our lives that wants to transcend this trap of isolation and fear.

What we know today from the modern sciences is that evolution is our fundamental reality. All of nature, in a sense, is summed up in the human person; the principles of nature are the fundamental principles of human personhood. Systems of nature work in tandem with the environment, so that when environmental conditions thwart the optimization of life, the system finds the necessary tools to adapt, change, or rearrange its organization. The maxim of nature is *life seeks more life*. This maxim holds true on the human level as well as throughout all of nature, except we do not follow the principles of nature. Instead, we seek to control nature and direct its course of action. According to Genesis 1:26–28, we were given dominion over nature, giving rise to the idea that the human person is special and distinct from nature. But the fact is, earth is *the* primary reality and we are derivative of earthly life. God was creating long before we arrived on the scene. We are not meant to control nature, but instead to be its mind and heart as it seeks its ultimate fulfillment. If we seek to manipulate nature, it will rise up against us.

The narrative of nature can be summed up in one word: *evolution.* We are evolutionary nature on the level of self-consciousness. Evolution works according to many factors, far beyond the simple rules of Charles Darwin, and one of the most significant factors is information. Evolution is a function of information and complexity; an increase in complexity corresponds to a rise in consciousness. It is no surprise that we find ourselves today in a massive shift of consciousness. The development of computer technology has drastically increased the amount of information in the human sphere. As a result, consciousness has rapidly com-plexified, giving rise to new integrated levels that can now be identified as global consciousness and planetary conscious-ness. While computer technology has enhanced the rate of evolution, most human support systems, including religious, educational, and political systems, are still structured accord-ing to a static, fixed model of closed systems, the Newtonian paradigm of the autonomous individual. Hence, the informa-tion-driven person who is electronically connected is living from an evolutionary open-system consciousness, while the support systems are individuated, closed systems. To continue this trajectory is to anticipate global breakdown. Newtonian systems can no longer sustain human life. Without rewiring support systems along the lines of complex systems, we are headed for global systems failure.

A seminal thinker whom I have relied on to navigate our unfolding world is the Jesuit scientist Pierre Teilhard de Chardin. As early as 1917 Teilhard could see a power at work in the physical universe despite the tragic reality of war and suffering. His faith and trust in the immanent presence of God impelled him to see the sufferings of the world as a breaking through of a new reality; neither war, nor communism, nor the loss of his family members prevented him from seeing the world in a dawning light. His optimism was balanced by a moderate realism that evolution must be the starting point for all human thinking, whether in religion, politics, or education. He indicated that dialogue alone is insufficient to move us to a new level of consciousness. What is needed is a new synthesis that emerges from the insights of science and religion. Evolution, he maintained, is neither a theory nor a particular fact but a "dimension" to which all thinking in whatever area must conform. The human person emerges out of billions of years of evolution. To realize that humans are part of a larger process, which involves long spans of developmental time, brings a massive change to all of our knowledge and beliefs.

Teilhard was convinced that the total material universe is in movement toward a greater unified convergence. As life systems unite and form more complex relationships, consciousness rises. Teilhard describes evolution as the rise of consciousness toward a hyper-personalized organism, what he called an irreversible personalizing universe. He spoke of the human person as a co-creator. God evolves the universe and brings it to its completion through the human person. Before the human emerged, Teilhard says, it was natural selection that set the course of morphogenesis; after humans it is the power of invention that begins to grasp the evolutionary reins. The computer, according to Teilhard, has evoked a new level of shared consciousness, a level of cybernetic mind giving rise to a field of global mind through interconnecting pathways. Technology is a new evolutionary means of convergence; it is accelerating evolution by causing humankind to concentrate upon itself through complex levels of information.

Teilhard penned his ideas almost a hundred years ago, yet he often has been dismissed as irrelevant, a charlatan. He sought to redefine faith within a scientific milieu. He challenged the church to accept the implications of the incarnation and to relinquish its otherworldliness. His ideas have been met with skepticism and only partially accepted. The Catholic Church remains fixated on the theology of Saint Thomas Aquinas, a brilliant theologian who developed his ideas in the thirteenth century. Although science has undergone three major paradigm shifts since the Middle Ages, the church still relies on medieval theology to explain the mysteries of Christian faith. While Vatican II opened the doors of the church to the world, theology remains distant from science.

Raimon Panikkar, in *The Rhythm of Being,* writes that theology and cosmology are interlocking disciplines. God and cosmos cannot be separated. Reality is radically relational and interdependent, so that every reality is constitutively connected to all other realities, is nothing but relatedness. The world of matter, energy, space and time is our home. There is an organic unity, a dynamic process, where every part of the whole participates in or mirrors the whole, including God. These realities are ultimate and irreducible. There is no thought, prayer, or action that is not radically cosmic in its foundations, expressions, and effects. Hence, there is no sacredness apart from the secularity of the world. The mistake of Western thought, Panikkar says, was to begin with identifying God as the Supreme Being, which resulted in God being turned into a human projection. But the divine dimension of reality is not an object of human knowledge; it is, rather, the depth-dimension to everything that exists. Panikkar called this complex reality a *cosmotheandric whole,* in which divinity, humanity, and cosmos form a trinitarian reality.

By insisting on Scholastic theology as the basis of religious thinking, religion has cut itself off from the related disciplines of science and philosophy. Today we have three loosely related disciplines—theology, philosophy, and science—each with its own methods, language, and concepts. Instead of having a cosmo-religious myth to provide meaning and purpose to human life, we have independent myths of science, religion, and philosophy. We can study each area and get a degree in one particular area without ever having to think about the other two areas. God remains locked up in Scholastic categories rather than being encountered as the immanent ground of dynamic being and cosmic life. To separate theology from science and philosophy is to destroy the cosmic genetic code. By keeping these disciplines distinct and apart, life cannot develop coherently, as a whole.

We have an urgent need to construct a new religious story today; theology can no longer be content to roam around the Patristic and Middle Ages while importing ancient ideas into the twenty-first century. We have confused history with a living God. A theology that does not begin with evolution and the story of the universe is a useless fabrication. Teilhard de Chardin felt the urgency to articulate his challenging ideas. His cry, "unify or annihilate," builds on a search for cosmotheandric wholeness in our dynamic world of evolution. His profound insights help us realize that a new story of the cosmos demands a new understanding of God, and a new understanding of ourselves in relation to God. Simply put, we cannot speak of God apart from human evolution, an idea that led Teilhard to state that God and world form a complementary pair. God and world are entangled with one another to the extent that talk of God is impossible apart from talk about nature and creative change, and talk of nature makes no sense apart from God. If a unified God-world relationship is the heart of theology, then theology cannot be done apart from modern science. Without science, theology can easily become idolatry.

This book is a collection of essays written over the last few years to help form a new theological vision for a world in evolution. They were written for a broad, general audience, especially those seeking new meaning and purpose in today's world. The title of the book, *The Hours of the*

Universe, is meant to convey the idea that the universe is the new monastery, the place to find God. Just as in a monastery the recitation of the Liturgy of the Hours calls to mind the work of God in our lives, from the gift of creation to the sufferings we bear, so too the new monastery is the cathedral of the universe.

Each chapter begins with a poetic introduction that expands the Trinity into the arc of the universe. The name *God* points to the mystery of an unspeakable source of eternal love that flows endlessly from the divine creative heart into the mouth of creation, an eternal divine kiss that is, at once, a deep intimate presence (Word incarnate) and an erotic attraction (Spirit) toward ultimate transcendence and fulfillment.

My hope is that each essay can be a source of prayerful reading, a searching for the depths of God's intimate presence in a world of chaos and change, for we are not alone and have no reason to fear. God is doing new things, and our response in fidelity and love can bring forth a new communion of planetary life.

Matins

Awaken!
Our universe is grand and wide
It stretches like gum ready
To blow a bubble.

A universe indifferent to life
Yet the mother of all life.
It doesn't know that it knows
Until we arrive.

The We Universe
Is the
Me Universe and You Universe
We are the conscious voice
Of the universe
But we are not all conscious
Of the universe voice
Within us.

So we continue to stretch
And Fold
And Fight
And Forgive
Because the universe
Is not yet
A Uni – verse.
The Many Still Search for the One.

One day it shall be so,
however,
Sometime, ahead,
in the future.
And then we will know

The Source from
which we began.
For the End is
in
The Beginning.

1.

Living in a Wavy Universe

From the dawn of our species, what we know about the universe has come from the power of observation.

Robert Grosseteste, a thirteenth-century Oxford theologian, described the beginning of all physical life from light. One of his major works, *De Luce,* begins with God's creation, a single point of light, which, through expansion and extension, evoked the entire physical order into existence. The expansion of light replicating itself infinitely in all directions, according to Grosseteste, was the beginning of the world.

Grosseteste was not too far from modern physics. In 1916, Albert Einstein announced his theory of general relativity, in which he rewrote the rules for space and time that had prevailed for more than two hundred years, since the time of Newton. Newton's physics stipulated a static and fixed framework for the universe based on concepts of absolute space and absolute time, which were considered independent of one another. Instead, Einstein showed that space and time form a continuum and are part of the physical fabric of the universe. Einstein's revolutionary discovery was based on light and the equivalence of matter and energy permeating the universe.

A year after Einstein announced his theory of general relativity, he predicted that the speed of massive objects would distort space-time, sending out gravitational waves or tiny ripples reverberating in the cosmos that can both stretch and shrink. Until September 2015 the existence of gravitational waves had not been directly detected. Their discovery is truly remarkable because they were not seen but heard! Using powerful laser electromagnetic wave detectors, scientists could amplify the noise of the waves and measure them, like a stethoscope on the heart of the cosmos.

Black holes are collapsed giant stars. They become cosmic "sink holes" that trap light and matter. They have been believed to exist in the universe but until now there has been little evidence of their existence. The gravitational wave discovery is based on the cosmic migration of black holes. Scientists speculate that about 1.3 billion years ago two black holes swirled closer and closer together until they crashed in a furious bang. Each black hole packed roughly thirty times the mass of our sun into a minute volume, and their head-on impact came as the two were approaching the speed of light. The staggering strength of the merger gave rise to a new black hole and created a gravitational field so strong that it distorted space-time in waves that spread throughout space with a power about fifty times stronger than that of all the shining stars and galaxies in the observable universe. This is what scientists at the Laser Interferometer Gravitational-Wave Observatory (LIGO) detected in September 2016. They actually heard and recorded the sound of two black holes colliding a billion light-years away, producing a fleeting chirp, which was recorded. This was the first time in the history of the cosmos that the human ear could actually listen in on a new hotline to the most hidden secrets of nature. Dr. Kip Thorne, one of the leading scientists in the discovery, said that until now scientists had only detected warped space-time when it is calm. The detection of the black hole collision revealed another side of nature's gravitational waves that could be likened to the ocean roiled in a storm with crashing waves.

The discovery of gravitational waves is truly awesome. The fabric of the universe is like a trampoline that can stretch or shrink due to massive objects like black holes colliding, or like a mattress shaking when a sleeper rolls over, producing ripples of gravity or gravitational waves. This is no static universe; rather, our universe is a mysterious ocean of energy and matter in which space and time are interwoven and dynamic, able to stretch, shrink, and jiggle. Even more incredible is the confirmation of black holes, the bottomless gravitational pits from which not even light can escape. The discovery of gravitational waves now gives scientists a new opportunity to understand the early universe and the powerful cosmic events that created these waves.

But what does this mean for us? Well, on the macro level not much. Life goes on with its ups and downs, births and deaths, good days and bad days, failures and achievements. But on a deeper level the discovery of gravitational waves tells us that science is living between mystery and discovery. It is as if astronomers are listening in on cosmic oracles and not yet quite knowing what to make of the strange sounds. The elastic nature of space-time almost makes time irrelevant in the vast universe, which means searching for the origin of the universe may not be, as we conceived on the human level, looking back; rather, it may mean looking *forward*. The existence of black holes or massive star collapse also points to the eerie presence of death in the universe from which mysteriously new elements of life emerge and converge.

Einstein did not believe in a personal God, but he did maintain that mystery permeated the universe. Reportedly he said to one of his skeptical acquaintances, "Try and penetrate with our limited means the secrets of nature and you will find that, behind all the discernible laws and connections, there remains something subtle, intangible and inexplicable. Veneration for this force beyond anything that we can comprehend is my religion. To that extent I am, in fact, religious."[1]

The more we comprehend the universe, the more we see how truly incomprehensible it is. The mysterious new universe calls for a renewed sense of divine mystery in the cosmos, a new religious myth, a new narrative that draws us

---

[1] Walter Isaacson, *Einstein: His Life and Universe* (New York: Simon and Schuster, 2007), 384.

into these cosmic waves that are, in some fundamental way, the source of our lives. We need a new religious sense of time and eternity as operative in the moment of occupied space, not as future events but possible events. As pilgrims in this vast, dark, wavy universe, what do we hope for? It is time to take a few cues from science: (1) be ready to change the religious paradigm when the right time comes, (2) let go and let God, and (3) trust nature to generate new life. Scientists may treat mystery as mere data, but if we believe in matter as God's beloved dwelling place then we should trust nature completely because God is *in* the waves.

2.

Quantum Edge Catholicity

The discoveries of science today continue to astound us. For centuries we thought of ourselves as solid, fixed human beings in a stable, fixed universe. Now we must re-think ourselves as disco dancers in a bubble gum universe. Quantum physics has undermined all the great discoveries of matter from Aristotle to Newton, and we are now left with the wondrous reality of wave-particle duality.

This is not entirely news since quantum physics has been around for about a century; however, we thought quantum physics belonged to the elite group of scientists who study the fundamental levels of matter in dimly lit labs. After all, who can possibly decipher this weird world of energy except those with thick glasses who write indecipherable mathematical equations on chalk blackboards? In an insightful book entitled *Life on the Edge: The Coming of Age of Quantum Biology*, authors Johnjoe McFadden and Jim Al-Khalili, a molecular geneticist and a theoretical physicist, respectively, crack the code (so to speak) on how life in the universe emerged from seemingly dead inert matter into vital life-generating organisms. What was thought to be a specialty of physics now governs biological life as well.

Drawing on recent groundbreaking experiments around the world, *Life on the Edge* engages readers in a new understanding of biological life based on quantum mechanics, enabling us to understand, for example, how migrating birds know where to go, how we smell the scent of a rose, or how our genes copy themselves with such precision. Rather than mapping out causal connections and intricate pathways, the authors disclose the hidden ingredient of biological life, namely, quantum mechanics. What seems fine-tuned and designed actually flows out of complex energy fluctuations and quantum entanglement.

Almost all levels of biological life exist on the quantum edge, that is, the edge between order and random possibilities. Systems specialist Ed Olson explains that three billion years of natural selection have fine-tuned the evolutionary engineering to drive quantum systems to "dance" with the "noise" in the thermodynamic layer in a rhythm that is "just right" for maintaining life. Underneath the surface of structured existence, dancing energy fields support an array of activity between what we observe in the outer levels of life and what is actually taking place on the fundamental quantum levels. Our living cells harness the molecular "noise" in a middle strata to maintain their connection to the quantum bedrock. What is most amazing is that, as far as we know, there is only a single set of laws that govern the way the world behaves: quantum laws. The familiar statistical laws and Newtonian laws are, ultimately, quantum laws that are filtered through a type of lens or a middle layer of "discernment" that screens out the weird stuff.

In its evolution, nature has learned to create quantum states, that is, efficient, instantaneous, everywhere movement of the particles that can be harnessed at every moment. The emergence of biological life is like a giant Powerball lottery of random possibilities bubbling at every moment with built-in choices for optimization. The formation of structures emerges from, and in some ways influences, the ongoing choices of activity. Life thrives on the edge between stability and chaos, order and randomness—which leaves scientists baffled as to how this delicate balance between order and chaos is sustained. Recent research offers a hint that, instead of avoiding molecular storms, life embraces them, rather like the captain of a ship who harnesses turbulent gusts and squalls to maintain his ship upright and on course. As the physicist Erwin Schrödinger predicted, life navigates a narrow stream between the classical world of order and the quantum world of random energy in such a way that life thrives on the quantum edge.

The discoveries of science today are becoming more and more revelatory of an astonishing world. From a faith perspective these new and exciting discoveries are rendering the word *being* tired and limp, impelling a new understanding of existence that reflects the dazzling dynamic energy fields of matter. If quantum physics has staged a revolution of being, then what is God? Language falters as we approach the divine mystery, for God is more and more the ultimate energy of dizzying love, living quite comfortably on the edge between order and chaos.

We constantly pray to God to make order of our chaotic lives, but what if God is the very source of our chaos? What if chaos and disorder are not to be shunned and avoided but attended to and embraced? Nature shows us that life is not meant to be nice, neat, and controlled but lived on the edge between order and disorder. Perhaps what we need is not planned retreats but unplanned contemplation that can take place anywhere and anytime—the alert mind in a dynamic world.

Jesus was a "strange attractor"[1] in the midst of a chaotic culture, driven by the Spirit of love into radical relationships, dangerous choices, confrontation, and ultimately, self-sacrifice. His deep interior oneness with God expressed itself in a consciousness of the whole. Like Jesus, Christian life requires an incarnational commitment to living on the edge between the orderly known and the chaotic unknown of unlimited possibilities. Discernment is filtering out the factors impeding new choices amid random possibilities. Consciousness must

---

[1] The term *strange attractor* is part of chaos theory and refers to a basin of attraction with a system which can pull the system into a new pattern of order over time. See Ilia Delio, *The Emergent Christ: Exploring the Meaning of Catholic in an Evolutionary Universe* (Maryknoll, NY: Orbis Books, 2011), 26; Margaret Wheatley, *Leadership and the New Science: Learning about Organization from an Orderly Universe* (San Francisco: Berrett-Koehler, 1992), 121–27.

be centered on the whole of cosmic life so that randomness and wholeness are not opposites but quantumly entangled.

Our nice, neat doctrinal formulas and Sunday services blind us to life's chaos. We live in the controlled center of sheltered existence. We fear disorder and randomness; death frightens us. We want to maintain what we have, and at the same time we want a different world. This is not only impossible but unnatural.

The world of nature tells us that the flourishing of biological life rests on the openness of existence to new possibilities in the environment. Biological life does not work as a top-down control system but as a bottom-up/top-down interplay of informational flow, more like dancing a tango than building a house.

We can appreciate the new science intellectually, but quantum-edge biology challenges us to rethink how we organize our lives spiritually. The Spirit of God is within you, Jesus said: "The reign of God is among you" (Lk 17:21). We are not called to maintain the existing order but to engage disorder as it lingers on the edge of new order. This means living with a certain level of anxiety, uncertainty, and darkness but also with faith, trust, hope, and surrender. We are called to live with a renewed energy of love, gathering the fragments of life into new wholes and testing the possibilities of life with a sense of spiritual adventure. The life of Jesus continues to flow through the Spirit. Baptism and Eucharist quantumly entangle us with the energies of divine love, engaging us in the unlimited possibilities for new life.

The exciting discoveries of science render the church rather boring and staid at times. It does not have to be this way; neither should God be relegated to boredom. The Dominican mystic Meister Eckhart said: "God is the newest thing there is, the youngest thing, and if we are united to God we become new again."[2] Eckhart intuitively grasped the import of a dynamic world with God in the midst of new

---

[2] *Meditations with Meister Eckhart*, intro. and trans. Matthew Fox (Santa Fe, NM: Bear and Company, 1983), 32

life. We need to learn to trust our intuitive compass in order to harness this love-energy for the purpose of new creation. Life on the edge is dwelling in the spaces of the unknown, the unlimited, the unloved, and choosing to know, to expand and to love. God thrives in between the known and the unknown, between uncertainty and hope, stretching forth into the world as our souls expand with new levels of consciousness. God does not save us from chaos because God is *the source* of chaos. We live in the midst of chaotic love, called to trust, hope, and endure, for from the heart of chaos God is doing new things.

3.

A Big Thinker for a Big Universe—Teilhard de Chardin

The great medievalist Étienne Gilson once wrote of Bonaventure:

> You can either see the general economy of his doctrine in its totality, or see none of it, nor would a historian be led by the understanding of one of the fragments to desire to understand the whole, for the fragments are quite literally meaningless by themselves, since each part reaches out into all the rest of the system and is affected by the ramifications leading to it from the synthesis as a whole.[1]

What Gilson wrote of Bonaventure could also be said of Pierre Teilhard de Chardin, SJ, who saw himself in the lineage of the Greek fathers of the early church. Teilhard was such a broad, integrated thinker that readers either see the economy of the whole of his thought or none of it. Like the early Greek fathers, he developed a cosmic Christology based on natural philosophy (science), scripture (especially the writings of Saint Paul), and faith in Jesus Christ. His theological vision emerged out of a deep, prayerful reflection on the dynamic relationship of God and world. Evolution

---

[1] Étienne Gilson, *The Philosophy of St. Bonaventure* (Paterson, NJ: St. Anthony Press, 1965), 436.

was much more than Darwin's natural selection. According to Teilhard, evolution and creation, cosmos and history, are complementary aspects of the *one* process of reality. Within his worldview three levels of perception may be distinguished: physics/phenomenology, metaphysics/hyper-physics, and mysticism. The object of perception, for Teilhard, is always the *entire* reality. He thought of the cosmic Christ as being like a tapestry of divine love incarnating the vast dynamic expanse of matter in motion. To grasp his ideas, one must follow the threads of his tapestry, which begin in his integration of faith and science.

Teilhard did not think in terms of "Sally" or "Sam" but of the underlying principles that could bring Sally and Sam together. His system of thought is more like the grand plan of a great cosmic cathedral than about what kind of stones should be used or where to get the cement. To understand Teilhard is to think in big, broad terms because he was trying to bring into a new single focus the dynamic presence of God in an expanding universe. Al Gore said that Teilhard helps us understand the importance of faith in the future. "Armed with such faith," Gore writes, "we might find it possible to re-sanctify the earth, identify it as God's creation, and accept our responsibility to protect and defend it."[2]

Teilhard's brilliant insights were born out of a sharp scientific mind and a deep Ignatian spirit. He was first and foremost a scientist, and he wrote about theological matters as a scientist, not as a trained theologian. In his words: "I never leave for an instant the realm of scientific observation."[3] He realized that the real path to truth must begin with concrete reality. He wrote his grand opus, *The Phenomenon of Man,* not as a work of metaphysics, still less as a theological essay, but simply as a scientific treatise. Yet anyone familiar with modern science would find his talk of an imperceptible

---

[2] *Al Gore, Earth in the Balance: Ecology and the Human Spirit* (New York: Houghton Mifflin, 1992), 263.

[3] Pierre Teilhard de Chardin, *The Future of Man*, trans. Norman Denny (New York: Image Books, 1964), 161.

psychic "within" of matter or spiritual energy or a teleologically directed evolution as scientifically suspect. Teilhard was aware of such suspicions; he encountered them and wrestled with them all his life. Elizabeth Sewell notes in *The Human Metaphor* that Teilhard's greatest contribution may be methodological. What Teilhard contributes is a renewed scientific methodology that connects science with *logos*, cosmos, and *eros*, in a way that influences the whole psychosocial order and the course of evolution.

It is precisely his approach to the material world as a science charged with faith in which Teilhard could see a new role for religion in view of evolution. His insights on consciousness and the "withinness" of matter seemed farfetched in his day. Today, quantum physics is beginning to realize the "hard problem of matter," namely, that one cannot think of matter apart from consciousness, that consciousness is fundamental to matter. Teilhard took his insights one step further by indicating that if consciousness is fundamental to matter, then religion is fundamental to evolution, because religion is a function of consciousness, that which gives form to the free energy of the earth. In his essay "How I Believe" he indicates that most people think of religion as a strictly personal matter. However, he rejected this view from an evolutionary perspective: "To my mind, the religious phenomenon, taken as a whole, is simply the reaction of the universe as such, of collective consciousness and human action in process of development."[4] At the social level, he says, religion expresses faith in the whole, manifested in individual thought or self-consciousness. If we are to progress or evolve, we must release ourselves from religious individualism and confront the general religious experience, which is cosmic and evolutionary, and involve ourselves in it.

Although he saw himself as a scientist, Teilhard also realized the need for new philosophical principles that could support the integration of faith and evolution. He worked

---

[4] Pierre Teilhard de Chardin, "How I Believe," in *Christianity and Evolution*, trans. René Hague (Orlando, FL: Harcourt, 1969), 118.

to develop a philosophy of love based on the dynamics of evolution and a phenomenological method of experience. His insights on love as the prime energy of the universe, following the law of complexity-consciousness, are woven throughout his writings and provide a metaphysical basis to his personalizing universe. The physical structure of the universe is love, according to Teilhard. It is in the framework of a love-centered universe that one must consider his comments on science, eugenics, and the sociopolitical movements of communism and fascism. While he rejected the destructiveness of these movements, he was fascinated by the capacity of humans to coalesce into a unified system of power. He wondered why Christianity could not tap into the same power of unification so that the whole evolutionary flow of biological life could be drawn into greater unity.

While Teilhard was a trained paleontologist, he did not agree with Darwin's theory of evolution. In Teilhard's view Darwinian evolution did not adequately account for novelty and transcendence in nature. He believed that the phenomenon of evolution is "something very different from and more than a mere genesis of animal species."[5] He saw the emergence of different species within a larger flow of cosmic and biological life. He was inspired by the French philosopher Henri Bergson and the notion of creative evolution. Bergson posited an "élan vital"—a vital impulse in nature—that led Teilhard to develop his concept of Omega. God is in the midst of the whole shebang. God is not supernatural but *supra-natural,* not above but within and ahead, the infinite depth and ultimacy of life.

Teilhard was quite critical of the "wooden" Scholasticism of his age and saw a church entrenched in legalism and dogmatism. He worked tirelessly toward a new theological vision consonant with evolution. According to Teilhard, nothing should deter us from realizing cosmic personalization

---

[5] Pierre Teilhard de Chardin, "The Energy of Evolution," in *Activation of Energy*, trans. René Hague (San Diego, CA: Harcourt, 1976), 362.

or movement toward the fullness of Christ, because we are moving.

Teilhard died a lonely man in New York City on April 10, 1955. Misunderstood, rejected by the church, and silenced by his superiors, he worked tirelessly until the end. He believed that a new synthesis of science and religion could give rise to a new religion of the earth, one that would kindle faith in the world, faith in God, and faith in the future. He lived in this unwavering hope.

Lauds

Who are You, O God?
Better yet, what are you?

You have a name but
I cannot see your face,
Or am I looking at it?

The philosophers say,
You are Being itself,
Necessary Being,
Being without contradiction
Not like the rest of us.

So you are not Us,
And we are not You.
But You are not You,
Without Us, and
We are not Us
Without You.

Strange is this mystery
O God.
A mystery that arises
within me.
For You are something
Of me,

And I am something
Of You.

You are the Eternal One
Growing in time,
And I am in time,
Growing into Eternity.

Perhaps this
Separation of terms
is an illusion,
like the Buddha said.

For if I did question who you are,
I would remain a mystery to myself
Forever.

4.

Can We Discover God Anew?

$\mathcal{I}$t is strange how consciousness is so much a part of us that we are not even aware of it. Awake or asleep, consciousness defines our existence. The most fundamental and essential aspect of human existence is virtually unknown. What is consciousness in relation to matter? Two main positions are on the table: the first, known as monism or panpsychism, claims that both the physical and mental are ontologically equal parts of reality and that one cannot be reduced to the other. They are both properties of one neutral substance, x, that is neither physical nor mental. A radical panpsychism asserts that all matter is a form of consciousness. The second position, known as dual-aspect monism, states that the mental and the material are different aspects or attributes of a unitary reality that itself is neither mental nor material. Between these two positions, philosopher Phillip Goff explains that panpsychism is the best explanation for our current understanding of physics:

> Physical science doesn't tell us what matter is, only what it does. The job of physics is to provide us with mathematical models that allow us to predict with great accuracy how matter will behave. This is incredibly useful information; it allows us to manipulate the world in extraordinary ways, leading to the technological advancements that have transformed our society beyond recognition. But it is one thing to know the behavior of an electron and quite another to know its intrinsic

nature: how the electron is, in and of itself. Physical science gives us rich information about the behavior of matter but leaves us completely in the dark about its intrinsic nature. In fact, the only thing we know about the intrinsic nature of matter is that some of it—the stuff in brains—involves experience. We now face a theoretical choice. We either suppose that the intrinsic nature of fundamental particles involves experience or we suppose that they have some entirely unknown intrinsic nature. On the former supposition, the nature of macroscopic things is continuous with the nature of microscopic things. The latter supposition leads us to complexity, discontinuity and mystery. The theoretical imperative to form as simple and unified a view as is consistent with the data leads us quite straightforwardly in the direction of panpsychism.

Although panpsychism is alluring in light of the primacy of consciousness, it does not adequately explain biological evolution. If consciousness is the foundation of materiality, how does it account for material attraction and emergence? How does matter complexify and give rise to higher forms of consciousness? If consciousness emerges from billions of subatomic consciousnesses (proto-mental properties), then how do these properties combine to form neural connections undergirding experience?

Wolfgang Pauli, one of early pioneers of quantum physics, asserts, "It would be most satisfactory if physis (matter) and psyche (mind) could be conceived as complementary aspects of the same reality."[1] This view is known as dual-aspect monism. By way of definition: *Two or more descriptions are complementary if they mutually exclude one another and yet are together necessary to describe the phenomenon exhaustively.* Dual-aspect monism excludes reductionism of either an idealist (the primacy of consciousness or

[1] Harald Atmanspacher, "20th Century Variants of Dual-Aspect Thinking," *Mind and Matter* 12/2 (2014): 245–88.

panpsychism) or materialist nature (inert matter and mind) while being necessarily incompatible with dogmatic physicalism and scientific materialism. Similarly, Carl Jung proposed a view of basic reality that does not consist of parts but is one unfragmented whole, the *unus mundus*, based on the complementarity of mind and matter. David Bohm spoke of mind and matter as different aspects of one whole and unbroken movement. Harald Atmanspacher writes: "Conceiving the psychophysically neutral domain holistically rather than atomistically, reflects the spirit of a corresponding move in quantum theory, which started out as an attempt to finalize the atomistic worldview of the 19th century and turned it into a fundamentally holistic one."[2] According to Atmanspacher, the Jung-Pauli dual-aspect monist position corresponds to a philosophical insight implicit in quantum theory, namely, that mind and matter form a complementary whole that cannot be reduced to parts.

Pierre Teilhard de Chardin held to a dual-aspect monist position. Life, he writes, is "a specific effect of matter turned complex; a property that is present in the entire cosmic stuff."[3] Teilhard considered matter and consciousness not as two substances or two different modes of existence, but as two aspects of the same cosmic stuff. From the Big Bang onward there is a "withinness" and "withoutness," or what he called radial energy and tangential energy. Consciousness is, in a sense, the withinness or "inside" of matter, and attraction is the "outside" of matter; hence, the energy of matter is both attractive (tangential) and transcendent (radial). In this respect Teilhard identified the core energy of the universe as love, which both unifies and transcends by way of consciousness. The greater the exterior levels of physical complexity, the greater the interior levels of consciousness.

In his essay "The Position of Man in Nature and the Significance of Human Socialization," Teilhard indicated

---

[2] Ibid., 285.
[3] Pierre Teilhard de Chardin, *Man's Place in Nature*, trans. Noel Lindsay (New York: Collins, 1966), 34.

that the universe orients itself toward intelligent, conscious, self-reflective life. Mind and matter are neither separate nor is one reducible to the other, and yet neither can function without the other. With this background in mind, it is easier to understand why Teilhard saw the human person as integrally part of evolution: we rise from the process, but in reflecting on the process we stand apart from it. He defines reflection as "the power acquired by a consciousness to turn in upon itself, to take possession of itself as an object . . . no longer merely to know, but to know that one knows."[4] Following Julian Huxley, he writes that the human person "is nothing else than evolution become conscious of itself." The human person is "the point of emergence in nature, at which this deep cosmic evolution culminates and declares itself."[5]

What is really interesting about this discussion on mind and matter is the way Teilhard saw this reality as the incarnation of God. He believed that without creation, something would be absolutely lacking to God, considered in the fullness not of God's being but of God's act of union. God and world are in a process of becoming a new reality *together*. The Hindu advaitic (non-dual) tradition holds that pure consciousness is divinity itself. If consciousness is fundamental to Being—that is, if nothing can exist without consciousness—Christians put a name to this personal awareness of consciousness/Being/Life, namely, God. If mind is already present in matter from the beginning, it is because God is present from the beginning. Alfred North Whitehead spoke of an organic, mutual relatedness between God and world. If God is creating the world, it is because the world is creating God; consciousness plays a fundamental role. The movement from unconscious matter to conscious matter, from unreflective matter to self-reflective matter and personal

---

[4] Pierre Teilhard de Chardin, *The Phenomenon of Man*, trans. Bernard Wall (New York: Harper and Row, 1959), 165.

[5] Pierre Teilhard de Chardin, *Human Energy*, trans. J. M. Cohen (New York: Harcourt Brace Jovanovich, 1969), 23.

experience is the birthing of God in evolution. A mindful material universe giving birth to God is a radically new way to understand the relationship between God and world and the world's future in God.

The dwelling of the Divine might better be understood as becoming conscious of our aspiration toward Mystery, because the Divine already dwells within us. Catholic priest Raimon Panikkar, whose Spanish Catalan mother and Indian Hindu father influenced his development of interreligious theology, writes, "There is in Man an urge, an aspiration to know the source of all knowledge, and by knowing this, all becomes known."[6] This aspiration of the searching mind finds its inspiration *from within*. The meeting of mind and heart is the "space" where the Divine dwells. God is the absolute depth of the seeker's self.

Entering into ourselves, we find the presence of Mystery in our dynamism toward that which we know not but that which draws us onward. This aspiration is a total movement of our being; to become conscious of it is to reach an awareness of the reality of God. On the entrance of the great Islamic temple of Harran, this inscription is written: "He who knows himself knows Allah." Similarly, the medieval German Dominican mystic Meister Eckhart wrote: "He who knows himself knows all things."[7] The knowing of the knower, the minding of the mind is not another knower or mind. The knowing of the knower is the unknowable, ineffable, inexpressible One, or as one Upanishad states: "It is not the mind that one should seek to understand; one should know the thinker." This is apropos to the problem of knowledge. We seek to understand the mind when in fact we should try to understand what is minding the "mind" or the One who is "minding matter." In the final analysis we are asking

---

[6] Raimon Panikkar, *The Rhythm of Being* (Maryknoll, NY: Orbis Books), 183.

[7] Cited in Raimon Panikkar, *Mysticism and Spirituality: Mysticism, the Fullness of Life*, ed. Milena Carrara Pavan, Part One (Maryknoll, NY: Orbis Books, 2011), xxi.

about that which is other than the known and beyond the unknown, namely, God. God is the unsayable reality at the heart of all reality.

5.

Mercy and the Humility of God

Recently, as I was rushing to catch the DC Metro, I tripped over my suitcase while running down a set of concrete steps and landed flat on my face. Actually, my chin bore the brunt of the impact. My plans that day came to an abrupt halt. I lay stunned on the ground, for a moment thinking that I had broken my jaw and that I would never speak again. I was not on the ground for more than a minute when I looked up and saw the face of a young man whose dark eyes were looking intensely at my ripped and bleeding chin. "Ma'am, are you all right? Can I help you?" He gently took my arm and lifted me up (only then did I realize that I had injured my knee as well). He notified the Metro police right away, and then he slowly walked me to a holding place in the station.

What deeply struck me, however, was the gaze of this kind man. I remember looking up from the ground and seeing his dark-skinned face with black-rimmed glasses. It was his eyes that said everything. He looked at my bruised face and asked, "Are you hurt?" It was not so much what he said but how he said it, as if in that moment I was the sole concern of his entire life. I was deeply touched by his compassion and care.

The gospel passage of the good Samaritan came to mind; in fact, it lit up my thoughts in a way that diverted me from the physical pain of my injuries. I had just met the good Samaritan of Luke's Gospel in Washington DC! He helped me up and brought me into the Metro police quarters; he waited with me until the ambulance arrived, assuring me that I would be properly cared for. The hands of time became the hands of love; he ditched his plans and waited with me for about forty-five minutes before I was whisked off to the emergency room. This young man, whom I had never met and whose name I still do not know, was in that moment a brother to me. I do not know if he was Catholic, Muslim, or of no particular religion. Nor did it matter. In the midst of being wounded, I saw in that young man the face of Jesus.

God Is Love

The medieval theologian Bonaventure described the incarnation as "the eternal God humbly bending down and lifting the dust of our nature into unity with his own person." Divine love is not an abstract concept; it is deeply personal, shown to us in the humble birth of a tiny baby. This mystery of divine love boggles the modern mind, whether it is the scientific mind of measurement, the intellectual mind of facticity, or the cultural mind of materialism. We cannot quite get a handle on what God is because we treat God like a concept.

Christianity sees the mystery of divine love in a particular way expressed in the person of Jesus Christ. Divine love is personally self-expressive and self-giving; the Word became flesh and dwells among us. Heaven has come to earth.

Bonaventure speaks of God as a fountain fullness of love, a love so immense that God bends low to embrace us where we are. The Victorine scholar Hugh of Saint-Victor, of the medieval school of Chartres, states that love surpasses knowledge; love takes us beyond the visible into the invisible and ineffable experience of unitive life. We know more by way of love than by way of knowledge because love is based on personal relationship and experience. To say that "God is love and those who abide in love abide in God and God abides in them" (1 Jn 4:16) is to say that experience and encounter trump conceptual ideas of the Divine. The Christian God requires the right brain of deep connectivity, passion, vision, and freedom. The emotional brain is called to connect through the senses: touch, taste, sight, sound, and smell. What does this divine Word made flesh call us to see? That the mystery of absolute divine love is absolutely given to us; divinity is relinquished into humanity (and the evolution of life leading up to the human). The gift is in the given, which means the source of All, Love unconditional, the Alpha and Omega, lies at our core.

Love Dwells Within

German philosopher Martin Heidegger spoke of Being not as a conceptual argument for God but as an activity immanent in this world, a self-giving presence rather than a transcendent creator God. In his view we are "immersed in a world of finite material things that we try to control for our own individual purposes but which in the end control us because we have lost perspective on how to deal with them in meaningful ways."[1] We accept without thinking the givenness of the world and most of the things within it. It takes an emergency, a break in our everyday consciousness, to become aware of what is always already there awaiting our response.

This may be the real import of the birth of Jesus, an awakening of consciousness to what is already present. Consciousness is awareness of what I am and what I am not, of what I have and what I desire. Philosopher Edith Stein states,

I do not exist of myself, and of myself I am nothing. Every moment I stand before nothingness, so that every moment I must be dowered anew with being . . . this

---

[1] Joseph A. Bracken, *Subjectivity, Objectivity, and Intersubjectivity: A New Paradigm for Religion and Science* (West Conshohocken, PA: Templeton Foundation Press, 2009), 110.

nothinged being of mine, this frail received being. . . .
It thirsts not only for endless continuation of its being
but for full possession of being.[2]

The "I" experiences loneliness only when it becomes unconscious of its very existence.

God is the absolute power and depth of the seeker. Delv-
ing into ourselves we find the presence of this Mystery in
our dynamism toward it. As we search outside ourselves
for meaning, we must search ever more within. In the total
movement of our being, and our becoming conscious of that
movement, we reach an awareness of the reality of God, who
dwells among us and within us.

Reflecting on the power of divine love in our midst opens
our eyes to the love that moves the stars and the other planets—the same love that gives birth to you and me. It is love
that lies at the core of our personal being and holds us and
the whole universe in being. In the words of physicist Paul
Dirac, "Pick a flower on earth and you move the farthest
star." Love entangles the earth and the stars. This love is
powerful and perfectly free. God is with us at every moment
with open arms, laughing when we are laughing, weeping
when we are weeping, rejoicing when we are rejoicing. God
shares in the brokenness of this world out of an abundance
of divine love. It is because God is the fountain fullness of
love that God can share in the sufferings of our lives and
through these sufferings draw us into new life.

Faith, Love, and Suffering

God's love is the power to heal and transform death into
life. To have faith in the God of unconditional love is to
realize how intimately close God is—so close that our joys

---

[2] Edith Stein, *Selected Writings of Edith Stein*, trans. Hilda Graef
(London: Peter Owen, 1956), 53.

and sorrows, our grief and anguish, are wrapped up tightly in God's humble embrace. So close we forget God's presence.

In his own day Jesus was immersed in a violent culture, a culture of conflict and anxiety. But he also knew of the deeper truth hidden beneath the surface of human judgment, namely, that this broken, anxious world is oozing with God. He asks us to have faith, to believe that the reign of God is among us and within us.

Jesuit Patrick Malone writes:

> Faith is more than a magical formula to conquer the worry, regret, shame and resentments that cloud our visions and make us jaded and tired. Having faith does not remove every trace of self-absorption and doubt. Those things are part of the human condition. Faith is what brings us into the deepest truth that says we are in the image of an unlimited, unrestricted, unimaginable love. And when we forget that, as Jesus reminded the religious authorities of his day, then religion does become a shield, a crutch, a closed refuge instead of a way to boldly throw ourselves into a harsh world, knowing that is precisely where we discover a generous God.[3]

There is no other path into the heart of God, as Bonaventure noted, than through the burning love of the crucified Christ. This may not make too much sense to us, especially in our own age of violence. But Cynthia Bourgeault captures the insight of Bonaventure when she writes:

> Could it be that this earthly realm, not in spite of, but because of, its very density and jagged edges, offers precisely the conditions for the expression of certain aspects of divine love that could become real in no other way? This world does indeed show forth what love is like in a particularly intense and costly way. But when

---

[3] Patrick Malone, "A God Who Gets Foolishly Close," *America* (May 27, 2000), 22.

we look at this process more deeply, we can see that those sharp edges we experience as constriction at the same time call forth some of the most exquisite dimensions of love, which require the condition of finitude in order to make sense—qualities such as steadfastness, tenderness, commitment, forbearance, fidelity, and forgiveness. . . . Let me be clear here. I am not saying suffering exists in order for God to reveal himself. I am only saying where suffering exists and is consciously accepted, there divine love shines forth brightly.[4]

The person who cannot love cannot suffer; such an individual is without grief, without feeling, and indifferent. To find in human suffering the liberation of love, and to love by accepting human suffering, is the path of costly, salvific love, where suffering is overcome by suffering and wounds are healed by wounds. We suffer the pain of suffering when we experience the lack of love, the pain of abandonment, and the isolation of unbelief. The suffering of pain and abandonment is overcome by the suffering of love, which is not afraid of what is sick and ugly but accepts it and takes it into itself to heal it. Is this not the way of mercy and compassion? Anyone who enters into love, and through love experiences the inextricable suffering of fragile humanity, enters into the human history of God.

That is why it is hard to explain logically a religion in which God gets absurdly close, so incredibly close that we are forced to discover the face of God in all the mess of the world, no matter how confusing or abrasive—racial injustice, terrorism, poverty, global warming. Too often we want a God who will hear our cries and fix things for us, who will be strong enough to push our painful experiences away. But the mystery of Christmas tells us otherwise. It is not that God is deaf to the cry of the poor. It is, rather, that God is poor. It is not that God does not see our tears, but God too

[4] Cynthia Bourgeault, *The Wisdom Jesus* (Boston: Shambhala, 2008), 99–100.

is weeping. Only a humble God who bends so low to pitch it all away in love can heal us and make us whole.

God has nowhere to dwell except in us, which means salvation requires our participation. The young Dutch Jew Etty Hillesum came to this realization as she awaited deportation from Nazi-occupied Amsterdam: She writes:

> All disasters stem from us. Why is there war? Perhaps because now and then I might be inclined to snap at my neighbor. Because I and my neighbor and everyone else do not have enough love. . . . Yet there is love bound up inside us, and if we could release it into the world, a little each day, we would be fighting war and everything that comes with it.[5]

Etty opened her heart to divinity and found God dwelling in humanity despite the atrocities of the Holocaust.

Compassion: The Arms of Mercy

This "bending low" of God, this "foolish nearness" of God, says to us that God lives in human hearts. God's compassion needs human hands, human eyes, and human touch. Our only credible action is to bless this world by allowing God to break through our less-than-stellar lives. We have enormous power to heal this wounded world through merciful and loving hearts, hearts that welcome the stranger and accept the suffering of another as our own. The Orthodox theologian Vladimir Lossky says that God is "a beggar of love waiting at the soul's door without ever daring to force it open."[6] Each of us must make a personal decision to open the door.

---

[5] Etty Hillesum, *An Interrupted Life: The Diaries of Etty Hillesum, 1941–1943* (New York: Henry Holt, 1996), 95.

[6] Vladimir Lossky, *Orthodox Theology: An Introduction*, trans. Ian and Ihita Kesarcodi-Watson (Crestwood, NY: St. Vladimir's Press, 1978), 73.

In my experience at the DC Metro I met a young man who must have let God in, knowingly or not, for he looked at me with eyes of love and compassion. In his face I saw the face of God.

6.

God in the Midst of Pain

As my spring graduate course on Christ and evolution was winding down, a graduate student in my class asked if he could write his final paper on Christ's descent into hell. At first I was reluctant because we had not discussed this topic during the semester. However, I gave him permission to pursue his interest, and I am glad I did because hell may be an apt description of the chaos of our age.

Today we learned of gun violence in yet another American city, and we can be sure tomorrow will bring news of more. Europe continues to teeter on the heels of Brexit, and conflict in the explosive Middle East shows no signs of abating. Fear reigns on every side, and one of the greatest signs of fear is the volatility of the stock market. The heightened fear of collapse—whether businesses or nations—impels people to take their money and run for cover. Our animal nature shows itself under conditions of external pressure and competition: either fight or flight.

Fear and fragility go together, and those who are fragile in their psychological and emotional makeup are having a difficult time holding life together. I once heard fear defined as deep hurt, and that may hold an element of truth. The human person is being threatened today on all sides. There is deep hurt, existential hurt stemming from lack of love and respect. Where there is no love, all hell literally breaks loose.

Pseudo-Dionysius, the profound fifth-century mystic, once wrote that God knows evil under the form of the good. This is a bit hard for us to digest, but I could liken it to riding in an airplane twenty-thousand feet in the air and looking down. One does not see tears and pain; one sees a quilt of rolling hills, deserts, and winding rivers. From a distance the earth is beautiful and bound in a web of goodness; close up, however, it is like a fragile piece of china cracking into many pieces.

God knows the beauty of the earth and the pain of the human heart. God bends low in love, to the furthest and most distant realms of life and death. This is symbolized by the cross, where we see most poignantly the poverty and humility of God. God's love is vulnerable and unconditional; it is love completely and totally turned to the other, willing to undergo death for the sake of life. Bonaventure wrapped together the mystery of love and suffering in his classic *Soul's Journey into God*. He writes that "there is no other path into the heart of God than through the burning love of the crucified Christ."[1] Anyone who enters into love, and through love experiences the inextricable suffering and the fatality of death, enters into the history of the human God.

For centuries the church taught that God is impassible, that God could suffer in his humanity but not in his divinity. This belief became difficult in the twentieth century when war—and all that war entailed—consumed millions of innocent lives. The German theologian Jürgen Moltmann tells how he lost friends and family to the violence of Nazism and how he would go to church and sit for hours before the crucified Christ, wondering what kind of God could allow such destruction. After years of praying before the cross he came to the insight that God really does enter into suffering humanity—and he wrote a wonderful book called *The Crucified God*. In it, Moltmann proposes a controversial, innovative way to approach Jesus's death, viewed as what he calls the "suffering of God." The distinction comes in understanding that the Son suffers on the cross, as "does the

---

[1] Bonaventure, *The Soul's Journey into God, The Tree of Life, The Major Life of Saint Francis*, trans. Ewert H. Cousins (New York: Paulist Press, 1978).

Father, but not in the same way." In a powerful passage on the suffering of God, Moltmann writes:

> When the crucified Jesus is called the "image of the invisible God," the meaning is that this is God, and God is like this. God is not greater than he is in this humiliation. God is not more glorious than he is in this self-surrender. God is not more powerful than he is in this helplessness. God is not more divine than he is in his humanity. The nucleus of everything that Christian theology says about "God" is to be found in this Christ event.[2]

For Moltmann, the idea of suffering is entwined in the act of love. Suffering is an indispensable aspect of God's life, one that is necessary to understand the power of God's selfless love. A God incapable of suffering would also be incapable of love. Such a God would be the God of Aristotle, a God loved by all but one unable to love at all. That is not the God of Jesus Christ.

Without love, God is forever unreachable. God's love is absolute and unconditional, and so too is God's suffering. God chooses to suffer in the same way that God chooses to love. Jesus chose to participate in suffering and gave his will up to the Father on the cross. The choice to participate in the pain and suffering of the world shows the sacrifice and love of God. In the cross the Father does not sit by idly while the Son suffers the pain and death. Rather, the Father participates in the Son's suffering, in the very act of God-forsakenness. God bears the pain of a parent watching his or her child undergo anguish and death. God enters into the human experience of forsakenness so that no violent act, no darkness, no pain is left bereft of God's love. God is there in the brokenness of heart, the tears, the anguish, confusion, and abandonment that forsakenness bears. Yet love is

---

[2] Jürgen Moltmann, *The Crucified God*, trans. R. A. Wilson and John Bowden (New York: HarperCollins, 1991), 205.

stronger than death. Even in the midst of darkness, God's love tenderly stoops down and embraces us, comforting us as a parent comforts a child, empowering us to get up again and choose life. When all has been stripped away in the pain of suffering, we can either die in despair or we can get up and live into a new future. God, who loves us in our darkness, is the power of hope, promise, and new life. When we are united to God, we become new again. To have faith in a God of unconditional love is to realize how intimately close God is. So close that our joys and sorrows, our grief and anguish are wrapped up tightly in God's humble embrace. So close we forget God's presence. In a world of anguish and suffering the lines between divinity and humanity become blurred. Jesus lived in a violent culture, a culture of conflict and anxiety, but he also knew the deep truth hidden beneath the surface of human judgment, namely, that this broken, anxious world is oozing with God.

We have the capacity for a new world and the capacity to destroy this world by failing in love. God will not clean up the mess we have made, but we are constantly invited into a new future. It is time to let go of everything we cling to and fall in love with Love. For Love alone can bring us to the threshold of another universe.

7.

Do We Make a Difference to God?

The realm of technology is our fastest game changer. In a mere fifty years we have gone from phones on the wall to computers in our hands, and soon we will have implanted chips and computer glasses. The speed of invention and delivery is both fascinating and frightening because we are not sure where we are going with our technologies or what we shall become. But the fact is we are becoming existentially dependent on them. What is it about technology that has come to define modern life? I presented this question to my class a few weeks ago, and one young woman said that technology has come to replace religion. Years ago, she said, people would pray and hope for better things to come, for new things to happen. Now, with a touch of a button, anything we want is at our disposal. Has technology usurped the place of religion? Do younger generations use technology as a means of transcendence? And if we have transferred our religious sensibilities to technology, are we aware that constant computer use is changing our capacity to remember, to think, and to love? Is our ability to act ethically changing as well?

For the ancients, to observe the stars and wonder at the vastness of the heavens evoked questions of meaning and purpose. The physical world had a central role in shaping their lives. Remi Brague speaks of the "cosmologization" of nature. To be human was to be drawn upright to contemplate the stars, to observe the movements of the heavens, so that the wisdom of above could govern the wise person below.[1] The harmony of the spheres governed the order of nature. The wise person acted in harmony with the whole of nature. The bond between cosmos and human endured up to the rise of modern science, when the discovery of heliocentrism and the movement of the earth disrupted the relationship between heaven and earth. Knowledge became detached from the outer world of the heavens and placed in the self-thinking subject.

Modernity brought with it a strange disconnect from nature; the human was observer of nature but not related to nature. While scientists mastered the details of nature, humans lost a spiritual connection to the cosmos. Knowledge became a means to power rather than a path to love; we forgot that we were made upright to contemplate the stars. By disinheriting the cosmos, we became lost in space, drifting for the last two centuries in an expanding universe.

Part of the cosmic drift is due to the fact that the scientific mastery of space pushed God out of the cosmos. For some, God landed in the human heart of inner spiritual piety; for others, God retired into heaven and governed from above; for still others, God simply disappeared. Ethics suffered the consequences of divine cosmic displacement. Immanuel Kant probably said it best when he exclaimed, "Two things occupy me, the starry heavens without and the moral law within."[2] What motivates our actions? Does God care what we do? Does it matter how we vote or if we reduce carbon emissions or if we care for the poor? Does it make a difference if we criticize others or malign their reputations? Do our actions make any difference to God? Those who hold to the Thomistic-Aristotelian position would say no, they do not. We are related to God insofar as we participate in God; however, God is not really related to us. Although we will

---

[1] Rémi Brague, *The Wisdom of the World: The Human Experience of the Universe in Western Thought,* trans. Teresa Lavendar Fagan (Chicago: University of Chicago Press, 2003).

[2] Immanuel Kant, *The Critique of Practical Reason*, trans. Thomas Kingsmill Abbott (Auckland: Floating Press, 2009 <1788>), 256.

have to give an account of our lives at the last judgment, our actions do not affect God's life.

Teilhard de Chardin, however, thought otherwise. First, he held that God and nature belong together; they are mutually affirming opposites. Second, he believed that creation was essential to God, that it contributed to God what was lacking in God's divinity, namely, materiality. Teilhard believed that without creation, something would be absolutely lacking to God, considered in the fullness not of God's being but of God's act of union. Teilhard proposed that union with God "must be effected by passing through and emerging from matter."[3] Hence, God and creation have a real relationship; what takes place in the physical world makes a difference to God. Teilhard addressed the artificial separation between theology and science in the same way that the Greeks attended to the whole of experience. By highlighting an inner spiritual depth to physical evolution, Teilhard cosmologized religion, broadening its biological function. The true function of religion is "to sustain and spur on the progress of life." Thus, the religious function increases in the same direction and to the same extent as "hominization," that is, the emergence and growth of religion corresponds to the growth of humankind.[4]

Teilhard held that God is at the heart of cosmological and biological life, the depth and center of everything that exists. God is within and ahead, the field of infinite possibilities; God's invitation (grace) activates or motivates our choices. God does not determine what is good for us; rather, God invites us to make choices. Our nature is already endowed with grace, and thus our task is to be attentive to that which is within and that which is without—mind and heart—so that we may contribute to building up the world in love. Every action can be sacred action if is rooted in love, and in

---

[3] Thomas M. King, *Teilhard's Mysticism of Knowing* (New York: Seabury Press, 1981), 66–67.

[4] Pierre Teilhard de Chardin, *Human Energy*, trans. J. M. Cohen (New York: Harcourt Brace Jovanovich, 1969), 44.

this way, both Christians and non-Christians can participate in the emerging body of Christ.

Teilhard argued that the work we do throughout our lives to improve our world is the primary exercise of our Christian faith. Since God is involved in evolution, our love for God requires cooperating with God's activity in building up the world. Sanctification means freely participating in this stream of life that is ascending toward fullness, that is, being incorporated into God's life in this evolving world. As Teilhard writes, "We will be saved by an option that has chosen the whole."[5] Illuminating Teilhard's ethics, Ed Vacek writes: "The moral upshot is that human activity is now necessary for the building of the world. No carpenter, no house. Without human beings, God cannot accomplish what God wants to accomplish." God uses and depends on our thoughts and affections in figuring out how to build the earth. "Put more sharply," Vacek writes, "the will of God is not an antecedent plan to be discovered by us, but rather it is a plan to be co-created through the exercise of our own minds and hearts."[6]

For Teilhard, centeredness and interiority are necessary for moral action because what we do makes a difference to God. Our worldly successes and failures make a difference to God. Whereas most biological evolutionists see human activity as fundamentally serving the propagation of genes, Teilhard sees this activity as contributing religiously to the pleroma of Christ. That is, part of God's perfection is to be related to all that is good. If God could not be really related to what goes on in creation, God would be less than perfect. Our lives and our work, therefore, fill out God's *relational* self. Thus, God receives into God's self the good that occurs in creation. Put poetically, Teilhard says, God penetrates everything. God thereby is also changed by the activities of

---

[5] Pierre Teilhard de Chardin, *Science and Christ*, trans. Rene Hague (New York: Harper and Row, 1968), 77.

[6] Edward Vacek, S.J., "An Evolving Christian Morality: *Eppur si muove*," in *From Teilhard to Omega: Co-creating an Unfinished Universe*, ed. Ilia Delio (Maryknoll, NY: Orbis Books, 2014), 159.

creation, so the traditional doctrine of the immutability of God is no longer appropriate. That is, when God relates to the world, a real relation in God is created.

The greatest significance of our work is that it affects God's own relational life. When we contribute to the building of the world and to developing ourselves, we make a positive difference to God's life. Teilhard's emphasis on the future has the salutary feature of making us responsible for the future. This orientation toward the future is missing in natural law, which advocates a moral order based on the divinely ordained good; however, natural law does not support an ethics for an unfinished universe. It provides a blueprint for rightness rather than promoting a concrete reality of becoming. The formula of natural law seems unnatural in view of evolution because it presumes a fixed law of nature despite the fact that nature changes. Teilhard's ethics is for people who are on the move. He proposes an ethics based on evolving into a future of more life, more being, and more consciousness—what he called ultrahumanism. He does not seek to maintain the status quo but to create an ethics oriented toward the future, which means nurturing the values that gather us in, bond us together, create a global consciousness and a cosmic heart. These values are not fixed; rather, they must be continuously discovered and discerned. The future is our reality; it is our common good. In short, Teilhard holds up the future as the basis of ethics in a world of change.

Teilhard's ethics for a world in evolution is not a willy-nilly playground of ideas. Rather, his ethics must be seen in the wider scope of Christogenesis. Our lives have meaning and purpose. We are created to participate in something that is more than ourselves; that is, we are made to contribute to the fullness of Christ and thus to help bring about the unity of all things in God. Just as the cells in our bodies make a difference to our bodily function, so too our lives make a difference to what the world becomes. We either help build this world up in love or tear it apart. Either way, we bear the responsibility for the world's future, and thus we bear responsibility for God's life as well.

8.

One Eye, One Self, One God

R aimon Panikkar was a Roman Catholic priest and one of the great mystics of the twentieth century. The son of a Hindu father and a Spanish Roman Catholic mother, Panikkar wrote of himself: "I left (Europe) as a Christian; found myself a Hindu; and I return as a Buddhist, without having ceased to be a Christian.[1] Influenced by advaitic (non-dual) Hinduism, Panikkar described the whole of reality as cosmotheandric; that is, cosmos, anthropos (human), and God not as three separate realities but as a totally integrated vision of the seamless fabric of the entire reality. This cosmotheandric reality is symbolized by the Christ, in whom divinity, humanity, and cosmos exist in a unified reality.

Panikkar lamented that our Christology was too small to meet the needs of our age. His real concern was the disconnection between faith in Christ and the cries of the poor, including the earth. Most Christians, he said, are apathetic regarding the problems of the world and are concerned with only their inner political polemics and private problems (married clergy, women priests, and so on). Consumerism dulls the human heart amid an ecological crisis, while a massive humanitarian crisis of poverty and hunger is ravaging many parts of the Third World. Panikkar points out that many people around the world live in subhuman conditions, thousands of children die daily due to human injustices, wars

---

[1] Raimon Panikkar, *The Intra-Religious Dialogue* (New York: Paulist Press, 1978), 2.

kill every day, and warring religion is still very much alive. His question, therefore, is what does contemporary Christology have to say about all this? What is the relevance of Christian belief to the burning issues of our times, and how does it relate to Christ? "A Christology deaf to the cries of Man," he writes, "would be incapable of uttering any word of God. . . . Christ is not a divine meteorite."[2] Christ is not a postscript to our otherwise comfortable lives. "If the mystery of Christ is not our very own . . . it might as well be a museum piece."[3]

The Greek title *Christ* is a translation of the Hebrew word *Messiah*, which simply means "anointed." The generic meaning of the word, "Anointed One," received a specific meaning within Judaism: the Messiah the people of Israel expect. The title was individualized in the person of Jesus, who was recognized as the revelation of the Christ.[4] In Christian revelation and through Christian experience, the Christian discovers the Christ. The incarnation, Panikkar states, is not only a historical act in time and space, but it is also a cultural event and only intelligible within a particular cultural setting. But the Christian incarnation is a universal human event, unless we reduce Jesus Christ to a mere historical being.

Panikkar centers Christ in the cosmotheandric Trinity. If we sever Christ from his humanity, he becomes a platonic ideal of perfection, an instrument of dominion and exploitation of others. If we break his humanity from his historical walking on earth and his historical roots, we convert him into a mere Gnostic figure who does not share our concrete and limited human condition. In Jesus, the finite and infinite meet; the human and divine are united; the material and spiritual are one. The humanity of Jesus is our humanity

---

[2] Raimon Panikkar, "A Christophany for Our Times," *Theology Digest* I39/1 (Spring 1992): 13–14.

[3] In Ewert H. Cousins, "Uniting Human, Cosmic, and Divine," *America Magazine* (January 1, 2007), 22.

[4] Raimon Panikkar, *Christophany: The Fullness of Man* (Maryknoll, NY: Orbis Books, 2004), 149; idem, "A Christophany for Our Times," 7–8.

as well. "Jesus is a sign of contradiction," Panikkar writes, "not because he separates me from others but because he contradicts my hypocrisy, fears, selfishness and makes me vulnerable, like he is.[5] Whoever sees Jesus Christ sees the prototype of all humanity, the *totus homo,* the full man—the new Adam.[6] Jesus Christ is the living symbol of divinity, humanity, and the cosmos (material universe) united as one—a *cosmotheandric* symbol.[7] If Christian faith is founded on a living, personal experience, we have to begin to make sense of Christ in the face of religious pluralism.

If "Christ is the central symbol of all reality," according to Panikkar, then in Christ are enclosed not only "all treasures of the divinity" but also hidden "all the mysteries of Man" (anthropos) and all the density of the universe. He is "the symbol of reality itself, the cosmotheandric symbol par excellence."[8] Like Teilhard, Panikkar relies on the Pauline theme: "For in him the whole fullness of deity dwells bodily" (Col 2:9). Thus he concludes, "*Jesus is* Christ but Christ cannot be identified completely with Jesus.[9] . . . Christ infinitely surpasses Jesus.[10] Christ is not only the name of a person

---

[5] Panikkar, "A Christophany for Our Times," 15.

[6] Ibid., 20.

[7] For a discussion on Christ as the cosmotheandric Mystery, see Panikkar, *Christophany,* 180–84; Cheriyan Menacherry, *Christ: The Mystery in History: A Critical Study on the Christology of Raymond Panikkar* (Frankfurt: Peter Lang, 1996), 117–20.

[8] Panikkar, "A Christophany for Our Times," 7; idem, *Christophany,* 147. See also Raimon Panikkar, *The Unknown Christ of Hinduism* (Maryknoll, NY: Orbis Books, 1981), 27, where he describes Christ as "a living symbol for the totality of reality: human divine, cosmic" or what he calls the "cosmotheandric reality."

[9] Francis D'Sa, "Foreword," in Panikkar, *Christophany,* xvi.

[10] Panikkar, "A Christophany for Our Times," 11. Paul Knitter writes: "Panikkar clearly states that no historical name or form can be the full, final expression of the Christ. Christ, 'as the universal symbol for salvation cannot be objectified and thus reified as a merely historical personage.' . . . Panikkar warns against an idolatrous form of historicism in Christianity," although he does recognize that Jesus is the ultimate form of Christ. See Paul Knitter, *No Other Name?* (Maryknoll, NY: Orbis Books, 1985), 155–56.

but the reality of every personal life, whether Jew, Muslim, Buddhist or atheist; that is, Christ does not belong only to the Jesus of history but Christ is the living human Person united with God at the heart of the universe. Thus Panikkar points to a deep inner center in the human person with the capacity to manifest Christ, what he calls Christophany.[11]

The term *Christophany* has as its root the *phaneros* of the Christian scriptures: a visible, clear, public manifestation of a truth. "Christophany stands for the disclosure of Christ to human consciousness and the critical reflection upon it."[12] Each person bears the mystery of Christ within. The first task of every creature, therefore, is to complete and perfect his or her icon of reality,[13] because "Christ is not only the name of a historical personage but a reality in our own life" (Phil 2:7–11).[14] To know Christ is to discover Christ within. This is where Panikkar and Meister Eckhart cross paths. Eckhart's famous words: "The eye with which I see God is the same eye with which God sees me" is a christophanic experience. In *Birth of a Dancing Star,* I wrote:

The "I" is wrapped up with God, like the double helix of a DNA molecule, in a seamless flow of life, in this dynamic complex of "God-life-my-life," embedded in the ongoing creativity of cosmic life. . . . Deep within the cave of my heart, a depth that belongs to me alone, I recognize a fire that burns brilliantly and glows with warmth. Through that glowing fire I see the outline of a face, the face of Christ, but I also see my face, and then I began to Christ's face as my face; and sometimes I cannot tell Christ's face from my face, and all at once I recognize a single face whose eyes are looking inward and outward. The word "God" simply doesn't capture this infinite depth of my soul that stretches towards

---

[11] Panikkar, "A Christophany for Our Times," 5.
[12] Ibid.
[13] Ibid., 21.
[14] Panikkar, *Christophany,* 21.

an endless horizon, which by its sheer unlimited being must be divine life because it is life other than my own and yet entangled with my own life. I then began to know that this strange thing called "self" that scientists want to convince me is nothing more than wires and chemicals embedded in a complex informational universe is something more than what can be measured. These wires and chemicals cannot explain my experience of this other-than intimate presence, which is me but not me because—in truth—I simply cannot account for my own existence. How can the configuration of wires and chemicals make a conjugate called "self" when in fact the more I try to know myself in this inward journey, the more I encounter another presence I call God, and the more I travel inward, the more God there is than self and, truthfully, the further I go the less I can speak of either God or self; there is simply an entangled fire of love. In the search for who I am I find God, and in finding God I find my "self" as no separate self but being itself flowing into and out of an unquenchable power of divine love.[15]

The more we enter into the mystical depth of our personal lives, the more we realize there is no "I" apart from a thou. The "I" or the ego is a contraction of self-awareness seeking to expand in this journey of life. God is mystery, and we too exist in that mystery. We are caught up in the "I-Thou" relationship of the Father and Son in such a way that, like Jesus, we too are the "thou" of the Father. We are entwined in the infinite "Thou-ing" of the divine fountain of love. Every human person manifests Christ because, like Christ, we are the children of God and thus are part of the divine outpouring of the Father. The Father is the source of my being, the mysterious Fountain of Being, so that everything

---

[15] Ilia Delio, *Birth of a Dancing Star: My Journey from Cradle Catholic to Cyborg Christian* (Maryknoll, NY: Orbis Books, 2020), 203.

that I am, including what I define as "mine," is pure gift. Everything is grace. In Panikkar's view I am not the ground of my existence, but neither does that ground exist outside of me. In other words, the ground is not an "other," a non-I but a "thou" an immanent transcendence in me—which I discover as the *I* (and therefore as my I) "I." I discover myself as "the thou of an I" ("God is the I, and I am God's Thou"). This is the genuine experience of Christian advaita or non-dualism ("not one, not two, but both one and two"), preserving both the interpenetration of identity and the reality of personhood. This divine indwelling, the inner fountain of every person's life, is an invitation to manifest the divine, to become another Christ.[16]

Every person is called to live from the inside, the "I-I" interabiding, rooted in our own deepest experience of spiritual seeking and finding. Christ then is no longer an external object of adoration but the deepest reality of every person's life, indeed, all life.

Panikkar states that the task of Christians today— "perhaps even our *kairos*—may be the conversion—yes, conversion—of a tribal Christology into a christophany less bound to a single cultural event."[17] By seeing the whole reality in the Christ mystery, he claims, every being is a christophany, "a manifestation of the christic adventure of the whole of reality on its way to the infinite mystery."[18] Christophany is a planetary Christology without dogmas or narrow stipulations; it is the root reality that binds us together.

---

[16] See Panikkar, *Christophany*, 78–82.
[17] Ibid., 162.
[18] Ibid., 146.

Prime

Creation flows from the fountain fullness
of creative energy,
Springing from a creative and dynamic Source of Love.
Relational, personal, generative, communicative
Love
Spilling over on the canvass of space-time;
Creation is like a song
That flows in the most beautiful of harmonies.

What could possibly account for such
Creative beauty bubbling up
Into life?
Could it be
The Beauty of Life itself,
A Divine community of Love?

Creation is a work of Art
And the Artist is a whole
Community painting
As I write.
Not one person but
Interlocking creative energies of
Divine Persons.
How could I possibly know this,
Unless I am somehow—mysteriously—
Related to the
Creating Persons?

Which makes me a personal
Created co-creator
Of an ongoing vision I can
barely detect.
But the vision grows within me
When my ego gets out of the way,
And I can see
For a brief moment,
A Radiant Wholeness
in Love.

9.

Teilhard's Christian Pantheism

Pierre Teilhard de Chardin was both a scientist and a careful observer of nature. His ideas on God, spirit, matter, Christ, creation, and redemption were not born in a chapel during Holy Hour or through committee meetings of highbrow specialists, arguing over whether or not the use of the word *infallible* should be applied to all teachings of the church. Most of his writings are based on careful and detailed studies of physics and biology. It is not surprising that, as a scientist and a Jesuit, Teilhard would be fascinated by matter itself.

In his essay "The Spiritual Power of Matter" Teilhard writes in a lyrical and mystical way of the power of matter, in which divinity is hidden. He awakens, so to speak, to the power of matter, surrendering himself in faith "to the wind which was sweeping the universe onwards." As he begins to see matter more clearly, his mind is illumined, matter reveals itself in its truth, "the universal power which brings together and unites." Every single element of the world begins to radiate divine love shining through the everyday stuff of the world. Teilhard claims we must suffer through the harshness of matter in order to know its radiance. He writes: "Raise me up then, matter, to those heights, *through struggle and separation and death;* raise me up until, at long last, it becomes possible for me in perfect chastity to embrace the universe" (emphasis added). On the highest level of union, Teilhard extols matter as the "divine milieu, charged with creative power . . . infused with life by the incarnate Word."[1]

In "Scientific Research as Adoration" Jesuit Thomas King brings together Teilhard's ideas on matter and scientific research. Teilhard came to realize the need to "wrestle with Matter" and see what it reveals, in the same way that scientific research wrestles with the world and comes to understand it in a way that someone who simply gazes on it never can. As King puts it, "Teilhard saw scientific research as essential to mysticism."[2]

According to King, for Teilhard, "science, like the mind itself," is "a process, always probing into the unknown." Mysticism therefore is not "contemplating a truth already established"; rather, "mysticism lay in the very act of discovery that create[s] a new truth." "It is in these terms," King writes, "that we must understand Teilhard's talk of loving God . . . 'with every fiber of the unifying universe.'" The universe is "in process," and one realm of the unifying process is "the mind of the scientist," engaged with the unfolding of the universe itself.[3]

"As scientists struggle to make sense of their findings," King writes, they are grasping for a new unity, new horizons of insight. "The 'fibers of the unifying universe' come together in the scientist's mind," as the mind is drawn to a power hidden in matter; for Teilhard this is "dark adoration."[4] It is "the supreme spiritual act by which the dust-cloud of experience takes on form and is kindled at the fire of knowledge."[5] Teilhard indicates that grappling with matter leads to "troubled worship." Entering the unknown dynamics of matter disturbs the known, including prayer and worship. It is not

---

[1] Pierre Teilhard de Chardin, *Hymn of the Universe,* trans. Simon Bartholomew (New York: Harper and Row, 1965), 70.

[2] Thomas King, "Scientific Research as Adoration," *The Way* 55/3 (2005), 28.

[3] Ibid, 29.

[4] Ibid, 24.

[5] Pierre Teilhard de Chardin, *The Activation of Energy* (New York: Harcourt Brace Javanovich, 1963), 9.

business as usual, for new knowledge leads to new insights, which leads to new visions and understandings, and in this respect, God continues to emerge in new ways.

For Teilhard, matter *is* the incarnating presence of divinity; God is present *in* matter and not merely *to* matter. This core belief is still foreign to Christian ears, for we pray as if God is not here but there, in heaven, awaiting our attention:

> I lift up my eyes to the hills—
> from where will my help come?"
> (Psalm 121:1–4)

In prayer we seek to "lift up" our weary spirits from the heaviness of matter, focusing our attention on God above. But the Christian God is here, in matter. Prayer is to lead us into the heart of matter.

Do we really believe that God is present in matter? Is matter the same as God? This would be pantheism, and while Teilhard leans in this direction, he is clear that God and matter are not equivalent. The preposition *in* is key. God is *in* matter, meaning that God is the ultimate horizon, the depth and breadth of matter, other than matter (transcendent) yet intimately present to matter (immanent). When everything can be said about a particular form of matter—for example, a leaf (green, veined, and its other properties)—we have not exhausted that which really draws us to it, such as its beauty or light. The ultimacy of this experience, which cannot be adequately spoken or described, is the presence of God.

So when Teilhard speaks of a power in matter, he is speaking of the ultimate power that eludes our ability to grasp or measure it. Yet it is a power that is deeply experienced and draws us into it, expressed in the many ways humans invent, create, and transcend themselves. Science, technology, art, music, study, writing are all forms of engaging this divine power in matter by which we transcend ourselves.

Unless we grapple with matter—not only in scientific research but all aspects of world-unfolding life—we are missing out on the power of life itself, the power we name as God. Twentieth-century science and technology discovered the hidden God of matter, but religion does not recognize "dark adoration" sufficiently to bring this hidden God to light. Hence, it is not surprising that people spend more time on social media than in church, or look to Google for answers to prayers.

People today are searching for something to believe in, a power that vitalizes and dynamizes life. If the God of Jesus Christ "fills all in all," as Saint Paul writes (Eph 1:23), then God must be found in all things. Teilhard thought that the church does not present Christ as filling all things but a Christ who is more Gnostic (known only by way of knowledge) or docetic (only in appearance) than incarnate. If faced with the Pauline cosmic Christ, he thought, many scientists (and engineers) would recognize this immanent power and presence as the God whom they had been finding in their work and worshiping with a dark adoration.

If the church could embrace modern science and evolution as the very stuff out of which God is born, then the unknown God would no longer be faceless, dark adoration could become luminous, and the need to become gods or superhuman would be met in the very act of worship.

The church is missing out on the most vital opportunity to reinvent itself for a world in evolution. God comes to light in human consciousness—becomes flesh—and shapes the world with a new power. Paradigms change because the universe is unfinished, and the mind is pulled to know, to form new horizons of insight. When the level of our awareness changes, we start attracting a new reality. Can the church be part of a new reality? There will no greening of the earth unless we truly belong to the earth and realize the body of Christ is within, groaning aloud in the pangs of new birth (cf. Rom 8:22).

10.

Lex Credendi, Lex Vivendi:
Laudato Si'

In 1967, historian Lynn White, Jr., wrote a provocative essay entitled "The Historical Roots of Our Ecologic Crisis" in which he blamed Christianity for the environmental crisis. Christianity, he wrote, with its emphasis on human salvation and dominion over nature, "made it possible to exploit nature in a mood of indifference to the feelings of natural objects." Because the "roots of our trouble are largely religious," he claimed, "the remedy must also be essentially religious. We must rethink and re-feel our nature and our destiny."[1]

Almost fifty years later Pope Francis wrote an encyclical that picked up where White left off: *Laudato Si' (On Care for Our Common Home)* is a work of breadth and depth. Pope Francis has paid close attention to scientific data that indicates that earth is in crisis. Global warming, water scarcity, loss of biodiversity, and other factors show that we cannot sustain a first-world lifestyle indefinitely.

Although we have known about an impending crisis for quite some time, we have done little to change our course. In 1990, a group of thirty-two distinguished scientists, including the late Carl Sagan and physicist Freeman Dyson, presented an open letter appealing to the world's spiritual leaders to join the scientific community in protecting and conserving an endangered global ecosystem. In that letter they assert, "We

---

[1] Lynn White, Jr., "The Historical Roots of Our Ecological Crisis," *Science* (1967): 1205.

are close to committing—many would argue we are already committing—what in religious language is sometimes called Crimes against Creation."[2]

A World in Crisis

A crisis is defined as a rapidly deteriorating situation that, if left unattended, will lead to disaster in the near future. Pope Francis has raised the planet's health situation to the crisis level. As a planet, we are in danger because the earth's systems are failing. Many scientists agree that global warming is real, that it is already happening, and that it is the result of our activities and not a natural occurrence.

We are already seeing changes such as glaciers melting, plants and animals being forced from their habitats, and severe storms and droughts increasing. Scientists predict that deaths from global warming will double in just twenty-five years; heat waves will become more intense; and global sea levels could rise by more than twenty feet with the loss of shelf ice in Greenland and Antarctica, devastating coastal areas worldwide. We are already experiencing some of these changes, and the bulk of destruction is primarily affecting the poor.

The encyclical of Pope Francis stands apart from his predecessors not only in its breadth but in its ecumenical and global appeal and its engagement with modern science. The many excellent conferences on science and religion sponsored by the Vatican have clearly influenced and informed the pope, not only on ecology but also on quantum physics, complexity, and evolution. There are signs of these sciences throughout the encyclical, and the pope's emphasis on interconnectedness indicates the need to move beyond the Newtonian mechanistic paradigm.

---

[2] Carl Sagan et al., "Preserving and Cherishing the Earth: An Appeal for Joint Commitment in Science and Religion," presented to the Global Forum of Spiritual and Parliamentary Leaders Conference, Moscow, 1990.

The pope highlights relationality as the foundation of all life, impelling him to posit a new metaphysics of relationship grounded in divine love. We are not simply human beings; we are human interbeings and share in the interrelatedness of all cosmic life. He writes: "Everything is related, and we human beings are united as brothers and sisters on a wonderful pilgrimage, woven together by the love God has for each of his creatures and which also unites us in fond affection with brother sun, sister moon, brother river and mother earth" (*LS*, no. 92).

Franciscan theology permeates the encyclical, and the pope raises up the patron saint of ecology, Saint Francis of Assisi, to new heights. Even Bonaventure is given ample recognition in this encyclical with his doctrine of exemplary creation, the deep relationship between Trinity and incarnation, and the resurrection as the transfiguration of all creaturely life. Describing creation *ex amore* (out of love), Pope Francis writes, "God's love is the fundamental moving force in all created things" (no. 77). This is a shift from classical theology, which posits that creation originated either by divine freedom (Thomas Aquinas) or divine will (Bonaventure).

Laudato Si' shows a deep Franciscan understanding of creation flowing forth from the heart of God, in which every creature expresses God in some way. The world is created as a means of God's self-revelation so that, like a mirror or footprint, it might lead us to love and praise the Creator. Francis of Assisi's beautiful "Canticle of Creatures" frames this encyclical with a passion for wholeness and unity in the overflowing love of God. Franciscans all over must be rejoicing that, finally, Bonaventure and John Duns Scotus are getting their due recognition.

An Inherent Roadblock

Laudato Si' opens with the words of the "Canticle of Creatures." This hymn, composed by Saint Francis of Assisi a year before his death, celebrates the glory of God resounding throughout the universe, the risen Christ whose life radiates throughout the cosmos through the life-giving Spirit. The nature mysticism of Francis of Assisi and the theological vision it inspired must be understood, however, within the framework of the medieval cosmos, a fixed, stable structure of orderly life with the earth as center.

As earth was center of the cosmos, the human person was center of the earth. The human person, created in the image of God, was the "noble center," as Bonaventure taught. The medieval person had a *consciousness* of belonging to a whole; *cosmos* and *anthropos* were deeply entwined. This kind of thinking led to a deep, integral relationship between the human person (microcosm) and the cosmos (macrocosm). In other words, the human had a role in creation: to reconcile matter and spirit in union with Jesus Christ.

The Rise of Modern Science

This consciousness of belonging to the cosmos changed with the discovery of heliocentrism and the rise of modern science. When Nicholas of Cusa and later Nicholas Copernicus proposed a sun-centered universe (heliocentrism), the church was not ready for the major upheaval of a moving earth. If the earth moved around the sun, then the human person was no longer center of a stable earth but simply part of a spinning planet. How could this finding be reconciled with the Genesis account in which the human person was created on the sixth day, after which God rested? How would sin and salvation be understood? From the patristic era to the Middle Ages, theology and cosmology were united. Theology, like philosophy, was not a particular science; rather, it was related to the whole. Cosmology was part of theology as long as the cosmos was believed to be God's creation. The rise of heliocentrism changed this God-world relationship.

The Separation of Science and Religion

The crises that Pope Francis highlights in *Laudato Si'* are not due to recent events; they have been at least five-hundred years in the making. We have become radically disconnected from one another because we have become radically disconnected from the whole, the cosmos. Nancy Ellen Abrams and Joel Primack expound the relationship between *cosmos* and *anthropos* in *The New Universe and the Human Future*. They indicate that a shared cosmology can help transform our fragmented world into a new unity: "There is a profound connection between our lack of a shared cosmology and our increasing global problems. We have no sense how we and our fellow humans fit into the big picture. . . . Without a big picture we are very small people."[3] Similarly, Pierre Teilhard de Chardin noted in the mid-twentieth century a split between the human person and the cosmos and claimed: "The artificial separation between humans and cosmos is at the root of contemporary moral confusion."[4]

This division between the cosmos (universe) and the human person has resulted from the split between science and religion. It is this split that Pope Francis is seeking to address in the encyclical because he realizes that we cannot go forward into a sustainable future without the insights of both science *and* religion. Thus he addresses the encyclical to *all* people of good will and states up front that "science and religion, with their distinctive approaches to understanding reality, can enter into an intense dialogue fruitful for both" (no. 62). It is precisely how science and religion relate, however, that is ambivalent in the encyclical.

---

[3] Nancy Ellen Abrams and Joel R. Primack, *The New Universe and the Human Future: How a Shared Cosmology Could Transform the World* (New Haven, CT: Yale University Press, 2011), xii–xiii.

[4] Pierre Teilhard de Chardin, *The Activation of Energy* (New York: Harcourt Brace Javanovich, 1963), 80.

Old and New Creation

Laudato Si' supports evolution without explicitly saying so. The Pope writes that God is "creating a world *in need of development*" (no. 80, emphasis added), and God's role in this process is one of selfless love. Using the Jewish kabbalist notion of *zimzum* (divine withdrawal), the pope states that "God in some way sought to limit himself" in this creating process, thus allowing new things to emerge (no. 80). He sees God's love as "the fundamental force *in* all created things" (no. 77, emphasis added) and the power of love "intimately present to each being, without impinging on the autonomy of the creature," allowing creaturely life to unfold in freedom (no. 80).

Hence, Pope Francis points to a theology of evolution in this encyclical in a way that promises a new vision for the world. However, he reverts to an old theology when he states: "The best way to restore men and women to their rightful place, putting an end to their claim to absolute dominion over the earth, is to speak once more of the figure of a Father who creates and who alone owns the world" (no. 75). When it comes to the human person, the evolutionary paradigm is jettisoned for special creation and divine intervention. The pope writes:

> Human beings, even if we postulate a process of evolution, also possess a uniqueness which cannot be fully explained by the evolution of other open systems. . . . Our capacity to reason, to develop arguments, to be inventive . . . are signs of a uniqueness which transcends the spheres of physics and biology. The sheer novelty involved in the emergence of a personal being within a material universe presupposes a *direct action of God* and a particular call to life. (no. 81, emphasis added)

Francis reaffirms the position of Pope Pius XII, who writes that the human body may come about by way of evolution, but the soul is created immediately by God (see *Humani generis,* no. 36). Despite the fact that Pope Francis relies on Teilhard de Chardin— for example, describing the Eucharist as a living center of the universe, "an act of cosmic love" celebrated "on the altar of the world" (no. 236)—he affirms that "Christian thought sees human beings as possessing a particular dignity above other creatures" (no. 119).

Pope Francis seeks a renewed humanity, but a new humanity cannot be found apart from a renewed cosmology and a renewed theology. Raimon Panikkar reminds us that the name *God* is a cosmological notion, for there is no cosmos without God and no God without cosmos. In short, if our cosmology has changed, so too our theology and anthropology must change. These three realities—cosmology, theology, and anthropology—are so deeply intertwined that one cannot extract particular sections from any one of these areas or cut-and-paste and hope to find comprehensive meaning. They must be held together if they are to be understood together.[5]

The Vision of Teilhard de Chardin

No one understood better the implications of evolution for theology than Pierre Teilhard de Chardin. He indicated that dialogue alone is insufficient to move us to a new level of consciousness and new action in the world. What is needed is a new synthesis that emerges from the insights of science and religion. Evolution, he maintained, is neither theory nor particular fact but a dimension to which all thinking in whatever area must conform. The human person emerges out of billions of years of evolution, beginning with cosmogenesis and the billions of years that led to biogenesis. To realize that humans are part of this larger process, which involves long

---

[5] For more information, see Raimon Panikkar, *The Trinity and World Religions* (Madras, India: Christian Literature Society, 1970); and idem, *The Trinity and the Religious Experience of Man* (London: Darton, Longman and Todd, 1973).

spans of developmental time, brings a massive change to all of our knowledge and beliefs.

In the past Christianity had been above all a religion of order. The fundamental question Christians asked themselves was always the same: What is the significance of Christ in a world that was created in a perfect order but has been upset by original sin? The answer was unambiguous: Christ had come to restore the order destroyed by sin and to lead the world back to its original perfection. Now what we must ask is this: What is the significance of Christ in an evolving world, at the heart of humankind seeking its future?

By abandoning the doctrine of original sin, Teilhard was able to see the incarnation more coherently in its relation to creation, so that the mystery of creation and the mystery of incarnation form a single mystery of divine love. This world is not merely a plurality of unrelated things but a true unity, a cosmos, centered in Christ, who is the purpose of this universe and the model of what is intended for this universe, that is, union and transformation in God.

Teilhard used the term *Christogenesis* to indicate that the biological and cosmological genesis of creation—cosmogenesis—is, from the point of faith, Christogenesis. The whole cosmos is incarnational. Christ is organically immersed with all of creation, in the heart of matter, thus unifying the world. Teilhard introduced a new understanding of Christ as the "Evolver," the power of divine love incarnate within, who is one with Christ Omega. He posited a dynamic view of God and the world in the process of becoming *something more* than what it is because the universe is grounded in the personal center of Christ.

Technology and the Noosphere

Teilhard was convinced that the total material universe is in movement toward a greater unified convergence in consciousness, a hyper-personalized organism, or an irreversible personalizing universe. Jesus Christ is the physical and personal center of an expanding universe, and the Spirit sent by Christ continues evolution in and through us. Teilhard saw unification of the whole in and through the human person, who is the growing tip of the evolutionary process. He spoke of the human person as a co-creator. God evolves the universe and brings it to its completion through the human person. Before the human emerged, it was natural selection that set the course of morphogenesis; after humans, it is the power of invention that begins to grasp the evolutionary reins.

Whereas *Laudato Si'* speaks somberly of technology and technocratic power (nos. 102–14), Teilhard saw the computer ushering in a new level of shared consciousness, which he called the *noosphere,* a level of cybernetic mind giving rise to a field of global mind through interconnecting pathways. He insisted that technology is a new means of (evolutionary) convergence; humankind is not dissipating but unifying by concentrating upon itself. We call this new level of consciousness *global consciousness* because we now have awareness of life around the globe in a way unprecedented in human history. But Teilhard also saw that this new level of global mind could give rise to a new level of shared being and shared consciousness, a new level of unity reflecting the emergence of Christ. In this way Teilhard saw that technology could further religion at the heart of evolution.

A Religion of the Earth

Teilhard felt that traditional Christianity is too aloof from the world—too much at odds with the natural religious current of contemporary humanity, a closed system of routinized sameness. He writes: "No longer is it simply a religion of individual and of heaven, but a religion of mankind and of the earth—that is what we are looking for at this moment, as the oxygen without which we cannot breathe."[6] He called for a new religion of the earth rather than a religion of heaven.

Religion, in Teilhard's view, is primarily on the level of human consciousness and human action rather than in institutions or belief systems, except insofar as these manifest and give direction to the former. In his final essay, "The Christic," he writes: "In a system of cosmo-noogenesis, the comparative value of religious creeds may be measured by their respective power of evolutive activation."[7]

The Church in Evolution

Teilhard had a vision of the church in evolution. He spoke of the church as a new phylum of Christian amorization in the universe. By speaking of the church as a phylum, he imagined a new christified humanity, bonded by love, that would amorize (from the Latin *amor*, meaning "love") the cosmos and kindle love in the evolving cosmos. Anchored in the cosmic Christ, the church bears witness to the living God as the life of the world and hence to its own life as the body of Christ in evolution. The mission of the church, therefore, is the christification of the universe and the personalization of divine love at the heart of cosmic life. In other words, the church does not exist for itself but for the world. Teilhard asserted that a new vision of the universe calls for a new form of worship and a new method of action.

Laudato Si' calls for new action, but this cannot be effective unless the action sinks its roots into a new consciousness of church and hence Christian life in evolution. Pope Francis wants the world to change, but he does not see that change must take place *within* as well. Unless we change the way we think and pray, we will not change the way we

---

[6] Teilhard, *The Activation of Energy*, 240.
[7] Pierre Teilhard de Chardin, "The Christic," in *The Heart of Matter*, trans. René Hague (New York: William Collins Sons and Co., 1978), 97.

act. Evolution, Teilhard said, *is* the rise of consciousness; as we begin to see self, God, and world in new ways, so too do our actions follow. Only when a new level of religious consciousness emerges will a new reality emerge. Conversion is essential, as the pope indicates, but it cannot be spiritual conversion alone. Rather, conversion must take place on every level of ecclesial life—spiritual, theological, structural, organizational, interreligious—until the world begins to feel the spiritual impulse of love at the heart of all life.

Laudato Si' opens the doors to a new world by challenging a selfish world of disconnectedness and calling all people to a new world of interrelatedness. But the church must model the very principles it promotes: mutual relatedness, inclusivity, interdependence, dignity of all peoples, shared resources and responsibilities, all creatures united together as brothers and sisters, woven together in the love of God. The church cannot be the great exception to the world but must be its chief exemplification.

11.

Pope Francis and Saint Francis

From the moment he stepped onto the balcony, gave his first blessing, and announced his new name, it was clear that Pope Francis was inspired by Saint Francis of Assisi. After all, who could not admire the little saint of Assisi who spoke to birds, preached to flowers, and called all creatures brother and sister? Francis of Assisi lived the vision of Pope Francis's encyclical *Laudato Si'*. A simple man with a big heart, Francis of Assisi communed in solidarity with all of life. He lived dispossessed and dependent on the goods of the earth and the generosity of people. What he received, he gave away, for he had only one aim: to follow the footprints of Christ.

Francis of Assisi inspired theologians to reflect deeply on the meaning of the incarnation. Both Bonaventure and Scotus did so with the aid of philosophy and Scholastic theology. Their rich theological visions are woven into *Laudato Si'*, sometimes hidden or interspersed with the work of Thomas Aquinas. To appreciate the Franciscan pillars of *Laudato Si*,' however, it is helpful to understand the main theological points described by the followers of Saint Francis.

Bonaventure's Creation

As minister general of the Franciscan Order (1257–74) Franciscan theologian Bonaventure drew the spirituality of Francis into a rich vision of interconnected life. He described creation as good, flowing from the Trinity of divine love. The material world is created by the triune God and is dynamic and relational. God grants freedom to creation without disrupting the divine intention to which creation is ordered. Creation, he believed, is like a beautiful *song* that flows in the most excellent of harmonies. It is a song that God *freely* desires to sing into the vast spaces of the universe. There is nothing that compels God to create. Rather, creation is simply the finite loving outflow of an infinitely loving God. The world exists by virtue of the free creative power of divine love.

The beauty of creation for Bonaventure is evident in the order and harmony of the things of creation. Creation is not simply a stage for human activity or a backdrop to human longings; rather, the whole of creation has meaning and purpose. It comes from God, reflects the glory of God, and is intended to return to God. Every creature is an aspect of God's self-expression; because every creature has its foundation in the Word, each is equally close to God (although the mode of relationship differs). Bonaventure views the world as sacramental. It is a symbolic world and one full of signs of God's presence. The world is created as a means of God's self-revelation so that it might lead us to love and praise the Creator.

God calls forth within this universe human persons endowed with the freedom to participate in this divine artistic splendor. Bonaventure saw the human person as the crown of God's created order. Matter has a drive toward spirit, but only one who is matter and spirit can unite the material world to God. It is for this reason, Bonaventure states, that the role of the human person is to lead creation back to God.

John Duns Scotus

John Duns Scotus was a Scottish Franciscan theologian who developed the vision of Francis of Assisi into a rich philosophical and theological tapestry. Scotus looked at our world and realized that because God is love, and perfect love is absolutely free, nothing created is necessary. God is like an artist, and creation is the work of divine art. Every single aspect of the created universe exists because of God's absolute freedom and because of God's unlimited love.[1] The very existence of creation attests to God's unlimited love; each being is uniquely created by the divine will of God. Thus nothing exists necessarily except God.[2] Because God did not have to create anything, all is gift and grace, which means the present moment expresses eternal perfection insofar as creation is endowed with creative potential for fulfillment.[3]

Love is the heart of Scotus's theological vision. Since everything has its origins in God, everything has its origins in love. Divine love is such that creation, incarnation, the sacraments, and gospel life all manifest a single divine intentionality. This intentionality is nothing less than sheer delight in being with the created order *precisely* because of its intrinsic dignity. This order of divine intention is first and foremost relational in nature. That is, the order of divine intention exists for the purpose of a personal relationship with the created order, a complete communion of divine and human natures. God acts out of love and divine generosity.[4] God's power is ordered and intentional love; the essence of Being is Love itself. God creates because God freely wishes to reveal and communicate Godself to others as the fullness of God's own Love. Since God is love, and perfect love is absolutely

---

[1] Mary Beth Ingham, "John Duns Scotus: Retrieving a Medieval Thinker for Contemporary Theology," *Custodians of the Tradition: Reclaiming the Franciscan Intellectual Tradition,* ed. Kathleen Moffatt (Aston, PA: Valley Press, 2016).

[2] *De Primo Principio* 3.21, in *John Duns Scotus: A Treatise on God as First Principle*, trans and ed. with commentary Allan B. Wolter (Chicago: Franciscan Herald Press, 1266), 52.

[3] Kenan B. Osborne, "Incarnation, Individuality and Diversity," *The Cord* 45/3 (1995): 22; Scotus, *A Treatise on God as First Principle*, in Wolter, xvii.

[4] Mary Beth Ingham, *Scotus for Dunces* (St. Bonaventure, NY: Franciscan Institute, 2003), 120.

free, nothing created is necessary. God is like an artist and creation is the work of divine art. Every single aspect of the created universe exists because of God's absolute freedom and because of God's unlimited love. The very existence of creation, therefore, attests to God's unlimited love; each being is uniquely created by the divine will of God. Scotus's emphasis on divine love as the essence of Being is manifested in his doctrine of incarnation, which is the supreme act of divine initiative, liberality, self-revelation, and intimate presence to the created order. Christ is first in God's intention to love, so whether or not sin ever existed Christ would have come.

Divine freedom expresses Scotus's sacramental/artistic vision of love and exalts the generous liberality of divine and human goodness. Reality is shot through with creativity and freedom from the first moment of divine choice to create this particular world to the smallest activity of human free willing. Scotus uses examples from artistic creativity, such as the artist or the musician, to describe divine creativity.[5] God is presented as the artist whose creative activity is radically free in the way an artist is radically free in the creation of the work of art. In this radical freedom of artistic creativity there is artistic integrity; that is, divine love remains constant and steadfast, whatever the human response.[6] Beauty is at the heart of Scotus's vision. Beauty is not some kind of absolute quality in the beautiful object. It is rather an aggregate (*aggregatio*) of all the properties of such objects, a unity and harmony of all that exists in relationship to one another and to God, a harmony of goodness, as Ingham describes.[7] It is the rich and manifold relationships of beauty that attract and

---

[5] Mary Beth Ingham, *The Harmony of Goodness: Mutuality and Moral Living According to John Duns Scotus* (Quincy, IL: Franciscan Press, 1996), 130–31. Scotus writes: "Sound . . . is more from the order of percussion than from the power causing the sound; indeed if it is not an harmonic sound, it is totally unacceptable to the sense of hearing" (*Ordinatio* I, 17, n.152 (5:211).

[6] Ibid., xiv.

[7] Ingham, *Scotus for Dunces,* 138–39; Ingham, "Retrieving a Medieval Thinker for Contemporary Theology," 1.

finalize the human experience of rationality. Divine beauty inspires and informs the human journey of love.

Scotus emphasizes the power of the human will to love. Freedom to love is the seed for creative beauty and manifests itself as choice. While love is at the heart of his doctrine, it is ordered and rational loving. How we choose and what we choose make a difference. Rationality is ordered loving. The person acts not unreflectively or because of any external constraint or condition that requires action of a particular sort but because of integrity; right action is thoughtful love. In this respect Scotus sees the human person as the artisan of beauty in the world and speaks of two orientations within the will: an affection for well-being and happiness, and an affection for justice (*affectio iustitiae*), that is, an orientation toward right loving and right action. Justice involves treating all persons and objects as they deserve. It is a stance toward reality.[8] The goal of the human moral life is the perfection of love, not only in regard to God but to all persons as having God-given value and to creation as a divine gift. It is not the intellect, therefore, but the will as the seat of love that holds the key to rational perfection. The fullest development of the rational person involves love and communion.

Pope Francis and *Laudato Si'*

Laudato Si' echoes many of the themes found in Bonaventure and Scotus. Creation is on the order of love and expresses divine freedom in love; that is, "the creating word expresses a free choice" (no. 77). The humility of God is shown in the notion of divine withdrawal, by which "God in some way sought to limit himself," making space in the divine life for creation to emerge. God is Creator, the primary cause of all that exists, but intimately present to each being, allowing each being its own freedom to creatively become itself. Pope

---

[8] Ingham, *The Harmony of Goodness*, 25–40; Ingham, *Scotus for Dunces*, 88.

Francis holds a panentheistic view of creation when he writes that we should "think of the whole as open to God's transcendence within which it develops" (no. 79). Although he employs here language of developmental time and unfolding beauty, it is clear that the emphasis is on divine transcendence and the absolute power of God to create. The divine decision to create and to impart freedom to creation should not underestimate the power of the Father "who alone owns the world" (no. 75).

Creation and incarnation are entwined, and there is a perfect fit between Christ and creation; the universe is oriented toward the fullness of Christ. Pope Francis writes, "The destiny of all creation is bound up with the mystery of Christ, present from the beginning: 'All things have been created through him and for him' (Col 1:16)" (no. 99). Like Bonaventure, Pope Francis states that all creation is transfigured and transformed by the risen Christ:

> Thus, the creatures of this world no longer appear to us under merely natural guise because the risen One is mysteriously holding them to himself and directing them towards fullness as their end. The very flowers of the field and the birds which his human eyes contemplated and admired are now imbued with his radiant presence. (no. 100)

Similarly, Bonaventure writes in a sermon (IX):

> Christ shares existence with each and every thing: with the stones he shares existence, with the plants he shares life; with the animals sensation . . . all things are said to be transformed in Christ since in his human nature he embraces something of every creature in himself when he was transfigured.[9]

---

[9] Bonaventure, *Sermo* IX, trans. Zachary Hayes, "Christ Word of God and Exemplar of Humanity," *The Cord* 46/1 (1996).

Bonaventure's theological vision with Christ as center is consonant with the vision of *Laudato Si'*: "The destiny of creation is tied up with the destiny of Christ" (no. 99).

While *Laudato Si'* incorporates language of modern science, the cosmology of the text is both medieval and modern. Pope Francis accepts evolution to an extent, like his predecessors. God creates a world in need of development (no. 80); human beings may be explained in part by evolution, but "the uniqueness of humans cannot be fully explained by evolution," and thus the pope "presupposes a direct action of God and a particular call to life" (no. 81). Here we find an echo of Pope Pius XII, who writes in *Humani generis* that evolution may explain how the physical body of the human person is formed but the church maintains that *the soul is created immediately by God* (no. 36). We are the lodestar of creation and "all creatures are moving forward with us and through us towards the common point of arrival, which is God" (*LS*, 83).

I do not know if Pope Francis read Bonaventure or Scotus before composing his encyclical, but I do know that what the pope envisions for the world is a Franciscan vision of creation. Maybe it is time we give Franciscan theology the attention it deserves. Like Christ, Francis of Assisi was a revolutionary of love, and revolutions leave nothing unturned.

12.

Warming, Warming, Gone! Who Will Survive Climate Change?

The environmental movement is not new. We have known for more than a half-century that anthropogenic disturbances are causing profound changes in the environment. In the 1960s atmospheric chemists described a steady rise in greenhouse gases; soil scientists told us that soils are eroding in many places more rapidly than they are forming; the number of disease-causing chemicals have proliferated; species extinctions are taking place as biodiversity diminishes; deforestation is worsening; and the list goes on. In 1992, a group of Nobel laureates and scientists, including Carl Sagan and Freeman Dyson, gathered to warn the human community of what lies ahead: "A great change in the stewardship of the earth and the life on it is required, if vast human misery is to be avoided and our global home on this planet is not to be irretrievably mutilated."[1] Now, over a quarter-century later, we are realizing that the chemistry of our planet is changing. Biological systems and geological structures that took millions if not billions of years to form are being altered or obliterated. The earth is critically ill.

We have known for a long time that our first-world consumer lifestyles are damaging the earth and that the

---

[1] Christopher Uhl, *Developing Ecological Consciousness: Path to a Sustainable World* (Oxford: Rowman and Littlefield, 2004), 123.

most vulnerable on earth, the poor, are feeling the effects of this damage. The ecological footprint first developed by Canadian ecologist William Rees indicates that the American footprint is about 23 percent larger than the earth can sustain. If everyone were to live like an American, it would take about six planets.

We could blame the politicians for not making the environment a priority on their agendas. Perhaps if Al Gore had been elected president, we would have developed more sustainable environmental policies. We could also blame technology and the power of technology to attain efficient production, but that too would exempt us from any wrongdoing. No, the problem lies as much within us as outside us. Indeed, the problem in the public forum begins in the personal arena. If it is a problem of politics and public policies, it is also fundamentally a problem of religion. A famous albeit controversial 1967 essay by Lynn White claims that the source of the environmental problems is religious in nature. Christianity, White indicates, with its emphasis on human salvation and dominion over nature, "made it possible to exploit nature in a mood of indifference to the feelings of natural objects." He argues that no religion has been more focused on humans than Christianity, and none has been more rigid in excluding all but humans from divine grace and in denying any moral obligation to lower species. We will continue to have an ecological crisis, he claims, until we reject the Christian axiom that nature has no reason for existence except to serve us. He writes: "What people do about their ecology depends on what they think about themselves in relation to things around them." Although White's argument raised concerns, his thesis highlights the need for religion to heal the wounds of the earth. "Since the roots of our trouble are largely religious," he claims, "the remedy must also be essentially religious. We must rethink and re-feel our nature and our destiny."[2]

---

[2] Lynn White, Jr., "The Historical Roots of Our Ecologic Crisis," *Science* 155 (March 10, 1967): 1205.

Shortly after White advanced his thesis, the Norwegian philosopher Arne Naess initiated an environmental movement known as *deep ecology*. Deep ecology is not explicitly religious in nature but it is an eco-philosophy, a philosophical inquiry that asks the deeper questions about the place of human life. Deep ecology is founded on two basic principles. One is a scientific insight that focuses on the interrelatedness of all systems of earth life together with the idea that anthropocentrism is a misguided way of seeing things. The second is the need for human self-realization. Deep ecologists suggest we learn to identify with trees and animals and plants, indeed the whole ecosphere, developing a behavior more consistent with who we are in creation and more geared to the well-being of life on earth.[3] While the search for a renewed human presence in creation is essential to revival of the earth's health, how do we come to stand deeply in this interrelated and created web of life? Here is where the question of religion makes a difference.

Despite the studies showing that institutional religion is on the decline, religious beliefs, whether explicit or implicit, are a fundamental driving force of human choice and action. Bracketing religion for the moment, environmentalist Bill McKibben speculates that by 2050 we will survive dangerous physical changes but eventually yield to restructured lives with smaller footprints. Cities will look different, public transportation will be mandatory in cities, all new homes will be energy efficient using alternate forms of energy, and carbon taxes will be standard. According to McKibben, we can survive the devastating effects of climate change.[4] However, I want to differ with McKibben. I do not think the First World will survive the dire consequences of global warming; however, I do think the Third World will survive and rebuild. Here are my reasons.

---

[3] Alan AtKisson, "Introduction to Deep Ecology: An Interview with Michael E. Zimmerman," *Global Climate Change* 22 (Summer 1989): 25.

[4] For more information, see Bill McKibben, *The End of Nature* (New York: Penguin Random House, 2006).

The Western world, the starting point for global climate change, is based on principles of the Judeo-Christian tradition. Made in the image of God, given the natural world for our use (with the mandate of stewardship or dominion), and destined for eternal life with God in heaven—all these have contributed to the notion of human exceptionalism. We are Godlike, wonderfully made, and specially endowed with the grace of God. Our true home is in heaven, which is above earth.

Following the lead of McKibben, I would like to speculate on how things might have unfolded if the Catholic Church had accepted the Copernican model of heliocentrism in the sixteenth century, human evolution in the nineteenth century, and the Big Bang universe in the twentieth century. What would religion look like if Thomas Aquinas were replaced by Alfred North Whitehead or Teilhard de Chardin? How might we relate to a God who is dependent on us, becoming ever more divine? What would church look like if we knew ourselves to be entangled with one another and all creatures of the earth? How would we pray? Who would Christ be in an unfinished universe? These unanswered questions have led to deeply repressed religious drives in the human person today. Western religion has simply refused to accept the insights from modern science as the basis for theological reflection. The Catholic Church skirts around the issues of evolution and quantum physics, and the Protestant churches run a spectrum from evangelicalism to liberalism. Science is a deeply neuralgic issue for religion. Whitehead wrote in 1925: "Religion is tending to degenerate into a decent formula wherewith to embellish a comfortable life. . . . Religion will not regain its power until it can face change in the same spirit as does science."[5]

Because religion refuses to change based on new insights from science, the deep religious drives, including purpose,

---

[5] Alfred North Whitehead, "Religion and Science," *The Atlantic* (August 1925).

meaning, and personal identity, need to express themselves elsewhere. Hence, they show up in consumerism, artificial intelligence and space exploration. Even if we destroy the earth with modern technology, we can build new technologies of information that will save us from our own demise and perhaps digitally immortalize us.

It is shocking to realize that less than 4 percent of people in the general population are familiar with the main insights of modern science. Most religion or theology classes are taught with no reference to modern science, which means theology is basically taught without any reference to the Big Bang universe or cosmic life. Science and technology can easily threaten the confessional religious person. Religion is so deeply rooted in the human psyche that it is not hyperbole to say that the greatest obstacle to reversing the trends of global warming is religion. Lynn White identified this core insight in 1967, and the churches ignored him.

Pierre Teilhard de Chardin knew this fact as well. He devoted his life to bridging science and faith, indicating that Christianity is a religion of evolution. He uses a phrase of Julian Huxley's—the human person "is nothing else than evolution become conscious of itself"—and adds, "The consciousness of each of us is evolution looking at itself and reflecting upon itself."[6] Thus the human person is integral to evolution, "the point of emergence in nature, at which this deep cosmic evolution culminates and declares itself."[7] Teilhard asserts that "we must love the world greatly if we are to feel a passionate desire to leave the world behind."[8]

Through his penetrating view of the universe Teilhard found Christ present in the entire cosmos, from the least particle of matter to the convergent human community.

---

[6] Pierre Teilhard de Chardin, *The Phenomenon of Man*, trans. Bernard Wall (New York: Harper and Row, 1959), 221.

[7] Pierre Teilhard de Chardin, *Human Energy*, trans. J. M. Cohen (New York: Harcourt Brace Jovanovich, 1969), 23.

[8] Henri de Lubac, SJ, *Teilhard de Chardin: The Man and His Meaning*, trans. René Hague (New York: Hawthorn Books, 1965), 22.

The whole cosmos is incarnational. In *The Divine Milieu* he writes, "There is nothing profane here below for those who know how to see."[9] Christ invests himself organically with all of creation, immersing himself in things, in the heart of matter, and thus unifying the world. The universe is physically impregnated to the very core of its matter by the influence of his superhuman nature. Everything is physically *christified*, gathered up by the incarnate Word as nourishment that assimilates, transforms, and divinizes. The world is like a crystal lamp illumined from within by the light of Christ. For those who can see, Christ shines in this diaphanous universe through the cosmos and in matter. He opposed a static Christianity that isolates its followers instead of merging them with the mass, imposing on them a burden of observances and obligations and causing them to lose interest in the common task. "Do we realize that if we are to influence the world it is essential that we share in its drive, in its anxieties and its hopes?"[10] We are not only to recognize evolution but make it continue in ourselves. He emphasized that the role of the Christian is to christify the world by our actions, by immersing ourselves in the world, plunging our hands into the soil of the earth and touching the roots of life. His deep secular humanism reaches the core of Christian life, which is a mysticism of action, involvement in the world co-penetrated by God. He held that union with God is not withdrawal or separation from the activity of the world but a dedicated, integrated, and sublimated absorption into it.[11] Before, Christians thought that they could attain God only by abandoning everything. We now discover that we cannot be saved except through the universe and as a

---

[9] Pierre Teilhard de Chardin, *The Divine Milieu: An Essay on the Interior Life*, trans. William Collins (New York: Harper and Row, 1960), 66.

[10] Pierre Teilhard de Chardin, *The Heart of Matter*, trans. René Hague (New York: William Collins Sons and Co., 1978), 210.

[11] Ursula King, *Christ in All Things* (Maryknoll, NY: Orbis Books, 1997), 93.

continuation of the universe. "We must make our way to heaven *through* earth."[12]

Thomas Berry, a "geologian" and Passionist priest who was influenced by Teilhard, said the renewal of religion in the future will depend on our appreciation of the natural world as the locus for the meeting of the divine and the human. We need a spiritual reconstruction, creating an attitude of mind within which the ecological and spiritual are one. According to Berry, we need a new type of religious orientation, one that must emerge from our new story of the universe, a new revelatory experience within the evolutionary process that is from the beginning a spiritual as well as a physical process. Berry calls the universe the "primal sacred community," the beginning of the new ecozoic age that is based on several factors:

1. The universe is a communion of subjects, not a collection of objects.
2. The earth is a single reality that can exist and survive only in its integral functioning.
3. The earth is a one-time endowment; there is no second chance. The human is derivative; the earth is primary. All professions must be realigned to reflect the primacy of the earth.
4. We need new ethical principles that recognize the absolute evils of biocide, killing of life systems, and geocide, the killing of the planet.

Berry, following Teilhard, calls for a reorientation of religious being in the world, a shift of our attention from the afterlife to this life, from spirit to matter, from heaven to earth. We must not collapse the divine into the immanent but see the divine in ordinary reality, hidden in the carbon and air and water we in the First World take for granted.

---

[12] Pierre Teilhard de Chardin, "How I Believe," in *Christianity and Evolution,* trans. René Hague (New York: William Collins and Sons, 1971), 93.

We need structural and pastoral changes in religious practices and worship, essentially a renewal of religion for a planet in crisis and in evolution. Basically, we need a new religion of the earth, one that celebrates interdependency, divine immanence, mutuality, and shared future (among other values). The internal theological divides (internal wars) of both Catholic and Protestant churches preempt a renewed religious sensibility that leads me to suggest that the future looks grim for the Western world, which is fundamentally built on Christian principles.

At the moment the poorest regions of the globe, largely in the Southern hemisphere, are experiencing dire consequences due to global warming. Most notable is the deforestation and stripping of the Amazon rainforest. Yet, the poor know how to live on very little; they are community-oriented and know how to share with their neighbors. Material goods are means and not ends for human flourishing. Religion itself is not an obstacle to working for the good of the earth; primal spiritualities consider the earth sacred. The Mayan farmer asks forgiveness of Mother Earth before creating a furrow in the ground to plant seeds. Meanwhile, the wealthy West has stripped many of the natural resources of Africa and South America. There is a resilience among the poor and despite the lack of resources, the will to flourish is deeply present. According to an article in *Time* magazine, efforts in Ghana and Kenya are being made to attract African entrepreneurs willing to invest in sustainable energy resources. If affordable and clean energy can take root in Africa and other parts of the world, in places robbed of a decent standard of living, then 2050 may look different from what McKibben describes.

Without a religion of the earth, a theology of divine immanence, and a spirituality of unity, the wealthy West (and East) may indeed be reduced to rubble. There is no guarantee that money can purchase a sustainable future, and yet we cannot continue to support our first-world lifestyles. We love our lattes, our Land Rovers, our jet-set lives, our lobster fests on sunset beaches, and our wine tours along the Rhine.

For those who still maintain religion in their lives, God is privatized, individualized, and removed from everyday life. For the rest, religion is marginally interesting to discuss or simply nonexistent.

Without a deep shift in our religious psyche, reducing the carbon footprint alone will be insufficient. I anticipate that the West will undergo profound suffering due to catastrophic events in nature, giving way to devastating financial losses and physical casualties. The Christian God is deeply involved in a world of change. To continue to deny a deeply relational God who may indeed be dependent on us for the full flourishing of life and to deny the intrinsic relationality of all earth life is to invite the calamities of global warming. Jesus said it best:

> "The kingdom of God is not coming with things that can be observed; nor will they say, 'Look, here it is!' or 'There it is!' For, in fact, the kingdom of God is among you. . . . Those who try to make their life secure will lose it, but those who lose their life will keep it. I tell you, on that night there will be two in one bed; one will be taken and the other left. There will be two women grinding meal together; one will be taken and the other left." Then they asked him, "Where, Lord?" He said to them, "Where the corpse is, there the vultures will gather." (Lk 17:20–37)

Death is imminent, entwined in the present moment of life. We have choices to make in this moment, and God awaits our decisions.

13.

Can a Renewal of Inner Space Help Heal the Earth?

At a workshop on *Laudato Si'* an engineering professor laid out the numbers on global warming, indicating that in the next ten years the warming trend will dramatically increase. Despite all the information available and the seemingly infinite number of workshops and conferences on the environment, our impending ecological crisis is getting worse instead of better. Fifty years ago historian Lynn White claimed that the roots of the ecological crisis are religious in nature. The primacy of spiritual reality over material reality has led to a mood of indifference with regard to the natural world. Because the roots of the problem are religious, White said, the remedy must be religious as well.[1]

What does he mean by the religious roots of the environmental crisis? White means that Christianity, by emphasizing spiritual reality over material reality, has rendered us otherworldly and somewhat indifferent about creation. With all but humans excluded from grace, Christians are decidedly anthropocentric. He named Saint Francis of Assisi the patron saint of ecology. Francis was a materialist who rejected the intellectual emphasis of his time (Neoplatonism) and focused on concrete reality. Francis found the otherness of God in the nearness of the leper, the splendor of divinity in the humility

---

[1] Lynn White, Jr., "The Historical Roots of Our Ecological Crisis," *Science* 155 (March 10, 1967): 1205.

of a flower. Francis's world was charged, as Gerard Manley Hopkins puts it, with "the grandeur of God." His world was a spiritual reality at the heart of the physical world, and this reality held a place for his soul to ascend to God.

In *The Pearly Gates of Cyberspace*, science writer Margaret Wertheim offers an insightful discussion on the paradigm shifts of space.[2] She suggests that the medieval Christian world picture had both a physical and spiritual realm. It incorporated a space for the body and a space for the soul. The physical and the spiritual mirrored one another, and the link between the two resided in the human person as the cosmic center. While the earth was physically at the center of the cosmos, surrounded by the heavens and the firmament of stars, humanity was the center of an invisible spiritual order.

The whole universe and everything in it was linked by a great spiritual hierarchy, the Great Chain of Being, descended from God. Humans stood halfway between the ethereal beings of the heavens and the material things of earth. As material beings with spiritual souls, humans were the linchpin of the whole cosmic system. The human person as the center of the universe did not mean an astronomical position, but rather the center of the spiritual and material orders.

Within this finite physical universe one could imagine room beyond physical space, since the cosmos was governed by the Primum Mobile, the outermost sphere of a series of concentric celestial spheres that formed the universe. Beyond the Primum Mobile and literally outside the universe was the empyrean heaven of God, which was beyond space and time. Both Thomas Aquinas and Bonaventure wrote their theological works in light of this cosmology of medieval space, and both insisted on the reality of an immaterial, nonphysical domain.

The rise of modern science brought with it the conquering of space. Between Aristotle and Einstein, a truly revolutionary shift occurred in our conception of space. For Aristotle,

---

[2] Margaret Wertheim, *The Pearly Gates of Cyberspace: A History of Space from Dante to the Internet* (New York: W. W. Norton, 2000).

space was merely a minor and rather unimportant category of reality. By the seventeenth century, space meant the "whole of reality," leaving no room for any other kind of space to exist. The concept gave rise to a bold new mechanistic philosophy that saw the world not as a great spiritual hierarchy but as a vast machine. Newton made space the formal background of the universe, the absolute frame of all action. Yet Newtonian space possessed no intrinsic qualities of its own; space played a secondary, subservient role as a backdrop for the action of matter.

Modern mastery of the physical world is shown in our scientific understanding of physical space. In the last five centuries we have mapped the whole of terrestrial space as continents, ice caps, and ocean floors have yielded their secrets to science. Our understanding of physical space now extends beyond our earth, to the moon and other planets. On the micro level, particle physics has been mapping subatomic space; neuroscientists are now mapping the space of our brains. It is a modern cosmological fact that the whole of our reality is taken up by physical space. And there is literally no place within this scheme for anything like spirit or soul to rise above the physical world.

Wertheim sees the conquering of space by modern science and the eviction of the spirit—both the divine Spirit of God and the transcendent human spirit—as the impetus behind the exponential rise of cyberspace. Just as medieval Christians believed in a physical space described by their science (natural philosophy) and a nonphysical space that existed outside the material domain, so too the advent of cyberspace returns us to a dualistic worldview. Once again we have a material realm described by science and an immaterial realm that operates on a different plane of the real. Cyberspace offers the space of infinite possibilities where the human spirit can soar. It is the new space of transcendence, the realm of the new empyrean heaven, now readily accessible by a touch of a button.

Wertheim's thesis is compelling, because the discoveries of modern science have centered on cosmological shifts and new understandings of space. Cyberspace is the new frontier of the spiritual transcendence that eludes the grasp of modern science. It is interesting that White wrote his famous article "The Historic Roots of Our Ecological Crisis" in 1967, around the same time Gordon Moore of Intel predicted that computing power would rise exponentially. Indeed, that prediction has come true. Computer technology has changed the landscape of modern culture, while the ecological crisis continues to deepen.

The truth is we need a spiritual outlet, a place to transcend ourselves through imagination and creativity. On the positive side, the church offers a place for the soul to ascend to God; on the negative side, this space is closed and bounded by the Dionysian hierarchies (the ecclesiastical and celestial hierarchies). The space of the institutional church is a patriarchal space with no room for democracy, mutuality, or shared power, all of which can be found in cyberspace. The church portrays heaven as the place of spiritual perfection; computer life sees the space of unlimited possibilities as virtual heaven. Cyberspace is an open "ecclesia" where gender, race, color, or creed make no difference whatsoever. One can join a networked community without having to argue or defend gender or patriarchy. In the infinite landscape of cyberspace we can transcend our prosaic lives defined by gender, race, and creed.

Technology has taken over the space of religion, and the trend will not reverse any time soon. We long to transcend ourselves, to strive for the more, to become different persons. Technology is no longer a tool; it is an existential reality. We in the Global North are computer-dependent in just about every facet of daily life. We created the tools of technology, but now the tools are creating us. The term *cyborg* symbolizes the new hybrid of human and machine organized by a new configuration of networked information.

Despite the lure of cyber transcendence, our souls are not at rest; we cannot find the peace we long for. Loneliness has increased in our cyberworld; we are more wired together than ever before, and yet we are lonelier. The human brain is literally changing with constant computer use. Studies show that constant computer use is enhancing the narrow left brain of logic and analysis to the exclusion of the capacious right brain, which is connected to the body and the wider world. The brain is a "use it or lose it" organ. By spending the majority of our waking hours in Googleland, we are becoming more forgetful, impatient, and narcissistic; even worse, our capacity to think is diminishing.

Yet the space of cyberspace, like the medieval heavens, is transcendent, alluring and spiritually seductive. We can find or become anything we dream or imagine online. Just as the saints of old imagined and undertook heroic sacrifices for the greater glory of God, we too long to become something different—but without sacrifice. The computer circumvents the arduous process of conversion by creating a "wormhole," a bending of space-time that enables ready access to other worlds. Our alternate lives are a mere click away, keeping us tethered to our devices. This cyber soul-space is much more enticing than planet earth because the infinite possibilities of cyberspace keep the flames of human desire enkindled 24/7. As a result, the *over* stimulation of our psyches leaves our souls *under* attended.

In a sense Lynn White was correct. Our ecological problems will continue to deepen unless we recognize the heart of the problem is the existential need for spiritual space. Our institutional religions do not provide a breathtaking openness for the human soul to soar. Teilhard de Chardin saw the problem early on. He spoke of Christianity as passive, resigned, and consigned to a cosmos that no longer exists. Because spiritual energy is vital to the evolution of life, Teilhard thought that we must reinvent ourselves religiously, and he set about his life's work toward this goal.

We have yet to realize, however, a new synthesis between science and religion, a type of religion that is at home in an unfinished universe. But this is the key to a renewed sustainable earth. By conquering physical space, science has unwittingly shown our deep need for religion. Our souls need a place apart from the physical world of everyday stuff, a place to stretch toward the infinite and wonder about things that do not physically exist. How we reconceive religion in a scientific age *is* the basis of a healing earth. Pope Francis is right to take the lead in this regard, but his spiritual wisdom is not enough. We need a complete religious revolution—to liberate God from the grip of Greek metaphysics, to liberate divine revelation from the institution of religion, to imagine a new heaven and a new earth. The Christian tradition has all that it takes to make this revolution possible. In a sense, Jesus initiated a new Big Bang: "I came to bring fire to the earth, and how I wish it were already kindled!" (Lk 12:49).

Computer technology should inspire us to rediscover religion—a technology of the spirit that deepens love, widens compassion, expands forgiveness, and radiates beauty; a democracy of the spirit open to healing and wholeness—in which sex, gender, or power determine relationships, only love.

But the power of newness comes from within. Science has conquered space, but it has not conquered the soul. The inner universe is still a vast expanse of infinite love and life. The religious imagination must be set free to realize that all that we seek in the outer life can be found in the inner universe, what the poet Rainer Maria Rilke called the "outer space within" where "through us the birds fly silently . . . [where] in me grows the tree."[3]

The heart is the space of unlimited love and thus unlimited power because at the center of the heart is the pure glory of God. If our souls cannot find a renewed spiritual space on earth, then we will face destruction, but this great suffering will be our gift. For in the fires of suffering, love is purified, and only a pure love can open our eyes once more to the gift of life. Then and only then will we remember the future memory is not of the past alone. Rather, it is our ability to reconnect with our birthright of belonging to a whole. To remember the whole of reality: past, present, and future. Without memory there is no future.

---

[3] Rainer Maria Rilke, *Inner Sky: Poems, Notes, Dreams*, selected and trans. Damion Searles (Jaffrey, NH: David R. Godine, 2010), 177.

14.

Beatrice Bruteau, Pope Francis, and Global Community

*B*eatrice Bruteau was not a superstar or a household name, although she could have been. Rather, she was a contemplative scholar who pondered the deep insights of Pierre Teilhard de Chardin and Sri Auribondo, among others. She had a unique combination of intellectual gifts—philosophy, mathematics, natural sciences, psychology—and she brought these gifts to bear on her penetrating insights on evolution and human becoming, which she described in several seminal books.

As I began to explore Bruteau's ideas on evolution and transcendent personhood, I could not but think of Pope Francis's encyclical *Laudato Si'*. The encyclical is multi-dimensional, spanning vast areas of science, politics, economics, and technology. Relying on data from the natural sciences, especially in regard to global climate change, the pope anticipates dire consequences for the human community, especially the poor, if we do not undergo a radical conversion and began to rethink our consumptive patterns and reorient our patterns of relationship. The pope clearly sees the consequences if we do not make a sharp turn toward interdependence and global community.

It is interesting that the pope quotes a wide range of thinkers, from Teilhard de Chardin to Romano Guardini, and builds on the green ecology of Benedict XVI and Saint John Paul II. If Pope Francis's encyclical were likened to a layer cake, the frosting would be rich and creamy, with twenty-first-century ideas on global warming, economics, and human ecology. Yet, it is disheartening that the encyclical does not mention a single woman theologian or spiritual writer, either present or past. In this respect Pope Francis could have benefited from the insights of Beatrice Bruteau. It is her vision that I would like to highlight here.

The Influence of Teilhard de Chardin

Beatrice is known as a Teilhardian scholar. Like Teilhard, she held that evolution is a process of convergence toward greater unity and complexified consciousness. The only way to think about anything, according to Teilhard, is to begin with evolution. Evolution is not background to the human story; it *is* the human story. It is neither theory nor fact but a "dimension" to which all thinking in whatever area must conform. Teilhard writes:

> For many, evolution still means only transformism, and transformism itself is an old Darwinian hypothesis as localized and obsolete as the Laplacean concept of the solar system or the Wegnerean theory of continental drift. They truly are blind who do not see the scope of a movement whose orbit, infinitely transcending that of the natural sciences, has successively overtaken and invaded the surrounding fields of chemistry, physics, sociology, and even mathematics and history of religions. Drawn along together by a single fundamental current, one after the other all the domains of human knowledge have set off toward the study of kind of *development*. . . . Evolution is a general condition, which all theories, all hypotheses, all systems must submit to and satisfy from now on in order to be conceivable and true.[1]

---

[1] Pierre Teilhard de Chardin, *The Human Phenomenon*, ed. and trans. Sarah Appleton-Weber (New York: HarperCollins Publishers, 1999), 152.

Teilhard and Bruteau realize that the new science impels us to adopt an entire new mindset, a way of identifying ourselves and others and perceiving the world. For Bruteau, we must begin with a consciousness of life in evolution before any talk of economic, political, and social arrangements can take place. "Anything else," she writes, is "premature, useless and possibly dangerous."[2] Evolution is the *starting point* for understanding all aspects of life.

Laudato Si': Old and New Thoughts

Although Pope Francis alludes to evolution and aspects of modern science, his understanding of the human person blends a Thomistic theology of creation (God as primary cause) and the modern science of evolution. He follows the 1950 encyclical *Humani generis,* in which Pope Pius XII writes that the human may come about through evolution with regard to the body, but the soul is created immediately by God (no. 36). Although the pope maintains a theologically moderate position in the encyclical, there is no real synthesis between science and religion; rather, aspects of modern science are interspersed with traditional notions of creation and personhood. He follows what Ian Barbour calls a dialogical model of science and religion in which dialogue within the disciplines of science and religion, as well as across disciplines, is needed for a comprehensive understanding of the ecological crisis.

Teilhard de Chardin recognized that theology and creation are deeply intertwined. The integral relationship between God and creation impelled him to go beyond dialogue to find a new synthesis between science and religion. God creatively unites with space-time matter and empowers the physical process of evolution toward conscious wholeness in love. Christianity is a religion of evolution.

---

[2] Beatrice Bruteau, *The Grand Option* (Notre Dame, IN: University of Notre Dame Press, 2001), 61.

Beatrice Bruteau and Evolutionary Personhood

Bruteau not only understood Teilhard's vision of Christianity and evolution, but she also contributed her own insights to fleshing out a new evolutionary understanding of personhood. Fundamental to her ideas is the new science of quantum reality, which basically tells us that interconnectedness lies at the core of all that exists. We are not individual substances but centers of activity, or, as Bruteau writes, radiating centers and not gravitational centers. Each particular person may be likened to a particle in which our radiating centers are waves of relatedness. At the most fundamental level, we are webs of energy, fields within fields, which means we are always connected to everything that comprises the world. We never act alone or think alone because the fundamental stuff of life is intrinsically relational; in our cosmic roots we are already one. Our thoughts and actions *do* something beyond what we can immediately perceive. We are not simply human beings; we are interbeings interacting in the great cosmic evolution of the Whole.

Although we are already one on the level of quantum reality, this oneness is in movement. Evolution describes the dynamic impulse in life toward more being and consciousness; however, life does not evolve smoothly across species or even within species. Many factors impinge on evolution, such as environment, genetics, history, and climate change. That which essentially *drives* evolution, according to Teilhard, is consciousness. Evolution *is* the rise of consciousness. This insight influenced Bruteau's thinking on humanity in evolution. Rather than accepting the human person as a given, she drew a distinction between an *individual* and a *person* based on the evolution of consciousness. That is, if evolution is the rise of consciousness, than an individual is an individuated existent with a less complexified consciousness of otherness, whereas a person (from the Latin *sonare,* meaning "to sound through") is one who has a higher level of other-centered consciousness. A person is a relational being who reflects a higher stage of self-reflexive consciousness and a higher level of evolution.

Bruteau indicates that evolution evokes a whole new understanding of the human person. She writes: "We cannot *look at* or *talk about* a subject. To do so is to convert it into an object. We must rather *noetically coincide with* our self by experiencing our own existence interiorly."[3] Building on Teilhard's primacy of love-energy, she indicates that a person is not an individuated being; rather, a person is the unbounded activity of freely projecting energies—what she calls spondic energy (from a Greek word meaning "libation"). Spondic energy does not originate out of thought or will; it is not the *act* of an individual. Rather, it comes from a deep, transcendent center, the still point where we are held in being by Omega. It originates spontaneously, arising only from itself; it is always free. A person is one who acts out of a spondic, self-gifting center; anything other than a spontaneous energy center of relatedness is not fully reflective of a person. To affirm another, she says, we need not sanction his or her behavior, especially if it is hurtful or evil, nor need we even like the person in the sense of personality or emotional attraction. "All these belong to the 'individual,'" Bruteau writes, "not to the 'person.'"[4] She indicates that only persons can enter into communion consciousness; individuals remain external to one another. It is this transcendence of the person over the individual that makes possible the communion consciousness of the new creation in Christ.

To be a person is to be a creative center of activity, always in the process of becoming and living toward the future. Bruteau expounds her ideas in her essay "Trinitarian Personhood," in which she writes:

Our "I," our personhood, is not a *product* of God's action, something left over after the action has ceased.

---

[3] Ibid, 51.
[4] Ibid, 54.

Rather it *is* God's action in the very actuality of acting. "We" are not a thing but an activity. This is why
God's activity of ecstatically moving out to us is an act
of coinciding with our activity, just as our union with
God will be our ecstatically moving out to God as an
act of coinciding with God's activity. . . . This activity
which we are and which God is, is the act of creative
freedom, of initiative, of self-originated self-giving.

Personhood is an ongoing activity that is dynamic in nature
and crucial to the future of evolution. Like Teilhard, Bruteau
held that the human person is evolution become conscious
of itself. A person is one in whom there is a higher level of
integral consciousness marked by a deeper level of relationality. She calls this higher level *neo-feminine consciousness* and
describes it as one of intellectual intuition and creative love.
She writes: "The wholistic outlook characteristic of feminine
consciousness has two aspects, both of which must be kept
in balance: a fundamental and ultimate sense of unity of the
entire human race—and even of all of nature—and at the
same time an attentive and appreciative sense . . . of each
particular individual composing that whole."[5] The level of
neo-feminine consciousness is community building because
it orients one toward others, making something new for the
future by relating to others through the energy of love or
goodness. It is a participatory consciousness. The communal
organism united by this consciousness is not a blending of
elements or seeing an anonymous crowd. It is a deeply personal consciousness of participation, "an outflow of positive
energy intending that life should become more abundant."[6]
    Evolution calls us into a new type of holistic conscious-
ness where things are first seen *together* and then as distinct
within this togetherness. Bruteau distinguishes a holistic
consciousness from a partial consciousness, or what she calls

---

[5] Beatrice Bruteau, "Neo-Feminism and the Next Revolution in
Consciousness," *Cross Currents* 27/2 (Summer 1977): 174.
    [6] Ibid., 179.

the "grid of partiality," a consciousness of separateness and alienation from nature (and one another); a utilitarian way of thinking that turns the means into the end and forgets the original aim. If we are to evolve into a more unified whole, we need a holistic consciousness. Beatrice Bruteau describes a "grid of wholistic consciousness" whereby the world is seen as a pattern of inter-independence, complementarity, cooperation, friendship, and creative joy. Knowledge is not hyper-focal, specialized information but drawn from a level of experiential elements synthesized into a intelligibility located in the Whole.[7] Even in human relations, and the moral and religious insights that guide them, holistic consciousness works by "both/and" methods, rather than "either/or," striving for inclusion of all and reconciliation of differences. This participatory consciousness finds delight in giving oneself freely and totally to the creative process of whole-making creatively contributing to it in a unique way.

Consciousness is the "motor" of evolution. In an open universe life is future-oriented and depends on the evolution of conscious energies; it is consciousness that, in a sense, holds the whole together. When consciousness is fragmented or dissipated so too is the whole. Bruteau follows Teilhard who realized decades ago that "nothing holds together absolutely except through the Whole, and the Whole itself holds together only through its future fulfillment."[8] As long as we insist on old, quasi-dualistic ideas on what is "physical" and "spiritual" (for example, "body" and "soul") and do not see that we are fundamentally energy-turned-matter, we will continue to live on a lower level of evolution, as competitive individuals, spiraling downward toward global destruction.

Teilhard saw that evolution has ushered in a new principle of relatedness, and Bruteau expounds this principle in terms of transcendent personhood. Science discloses a radically new

---

[7] Beatrice Bruteau, "The Whole World: A Convergence Perspective," in *The Grand Option,* 39–52.

[8] Pierre Teilhard de Chardin, *Christianity and Evolution,* trans. Bernard Wall (New York: Harcourt Brace, 1974), 71.

understanding of God and world in which human consciousness plays a significant role in shaping the future. Just as old wine cannot be put into new wineskins, so too, old ideas cannot be put into a new paradigm of the world.

A unified world is not possible without a radically new understanding of the human person. The old ways of thinking, including patriarchy, sexism, and discrimination, must be transcended with a new understanding of personhood as an evolving open system. If we are to have any real sustainable future, we must begin with evolution by which every person is emerging out of a cosmic whole. On a fundamental level of physical reality, we are already one, but on the level of conscious personhood we must respond from the center of creative love, acting toward communion, revealing the glory of God. Because God is our root reality and the future toward which we are moving, the many continuously become one and are increased by one. There is no ending of life in God, only beginning; thus life will always be more than what we can imagine, even in eternity.

Terce

Was Jesus of Nazareth God?

Can we really ask this question, as if we might ask,
What is the inside of matter?

The patristic giants put on their heavy
Philosophical armory to tackle
This question.
Some said, "Yes," Jesus was truly God.
Others said, "Maybe" but he was also
Human.
Still others said, the logic of natures
Demands a distinction of terms.
So the question became
Illogical,
A battleground of intellectual wits
And power.

A poor woman in a small village
Awoke every morning with the
words, "I believe."
She believed without logical arguments,
She trusted without formal distinctions,
She surrendered in faith,
Throwing herself wholeheartedly
into
The arms of God.

She did not ask the question,
She was the question and
And God was the answer received
in a heart full of love.
For the logic of God,
Is the logic of love,
And one who lives in love
Lives in God
And God lives in her.
This is the Christ.

15.

The Cosmic Christ

$\mathcal{R}$ ichard Rohr is one of the great vernacular theologians of our age. He has the gift of taking complex theological ideas and translating the core insights into the language of the people. In doing so, he has helped thousands of people around the globe come to a new appreciation of the mystery of God and the need for renewed spirituality today.

In *The Universal Christ*, Rohr takes up the mystery of the cosmic Christ and does so with passion. The notion that Christ is the firstborn of creation, the head of the whole she-bang from the beginning, was supplanted in the early church by the emphasis on sin and salvation. Saint Augustine, in particular, felt the need to formulate a doctrine of original sin in order to highlight the saving grace of God. By the eleventh century the need to explain the damage due to the sin of Adam and Eve became the principal reason for Jesus Christ. If Adam had not sinned, Christ would not have come. No sin, no Jesus. The reason for the incarnation, therefore, found merit in sinful humanity, resulting in generations of people focused on their faults and failings. Salvation through Christ meant being rescued from a fallen world.

It is rather strange that the reason God became flesh was to repair human damage. Such a reason belies the very nature of God as love. In the early church theologians like Irenaeus of Lyons and, to some extent Origen, engaged the question of the incarnation by considering it as a work of love. Rupert of Deutz did so in the eleventh century, and in the fourteenth century an explicit doctrine on the primacy of

Christ was formed by the Franciscan theologian John Duns
Scotus. Scotus said that God is love and, from all eternity,
God willed to love a creature to grace and glory. Whether
or not sin ever existed, Christ would have come, because
Christ is first in God's intention to love. And in order for
Christ to come there must be humans, and for humans to
exist there must be a creation; hence, Christ is first in God's
will to love and thus to create. The reason for Jesus Christ is
not sin but the fullness of love. This view is consonant with
the scriptures. As Rohr points out, the Letter to the Colos-
sians states that the Christ is the firstborn of creation (1:15)
and in the Letter to the Ephesians the author writes that the
mystery "from the beginning of the ages has been hidden
in God" (3:9). What God intended from all eternity was to
share God's life with a finite creature so that Jesus Christ
is present from the beginning of the universe. Everything
is christic, Teilhard de Chardin indicates; God's incarnate
love is the source and future of everything that exists. In
Teilhard's words: "There is nothing profane here below for
those who know how to see."[1]

How do we know this Christ of the cosmos? Should we
study cosmology or astronomy? Should we forget about
sin and human weakness? Should we simply try to love
more and hate less? Actually none of these suggestions,
Rohr states, will lead us to the cosmic Christ, the Christ of
the whole. In fact, the whole notion of the Christ can seem
detached from Jesus, as if there is this divine whole we call
"Christ" that seems to pop up in Jesus. Here is where I might
draw a slightly different distinction. When we say that "Jesus
is the Christ," we are saying that the humanity of Jesus is
one with divinity, the mystery hidden from the beginning of
the world (Eph 3:9). There is a particularity here, a *haecceitas* ("thisness") that cannot be overlooked. Jesus *is* the
Christ which means all that God is, is given to us in Jesus,

---

[1] Pierre Teilhard de Chardin, *The Divine Milieu: An Essay on the
Interior Life*, trans. William Collins (New York: Harper and Row,
1960), 66.

rendering a new understanding of God as relational, self-communicative, self-emptying. Could this be said of Buddha or Mohammed? No, at least there is no basis to make such a claim (nor do their followers make such a claim on their behalf). In and through the human-historical life of Jesus we come to know a different type of God from that the Jews or Muslims profess. Jesus called God "Abba," and his deep unity with God was expressed by a new energy, the Spirit of love. Hence, through the life of Jesus we see a new under-standing of God emerge as Trinity; it is the unified love of the Trinity (the plurality of divine persons in a communion of love) that forms the content of the symbol *Christ*.

The Christ, therefore, is not an abstract symbol but the communion of divine persons-in-love expressed in personal form. The real content of this symbol is shown in the life, death, and resurrection of Jesus, the Christ. So does everyone have to become Christian to know the Christ? Absolutely not. Christ is more than Jesus. Christ is the communion of divine personal love expressed in every created form of reality—every star, leaf, bird, fish, tree, rabbit, and human person. Everything is christified because everything expresses divine love incarnate. However, Jesus Christ is the "thisness" of God, so what Jesus is by nature everything else is by grace (divine love). We are not God, but every single person is born out of the love of God, expresses this love in his or her unique personal form, and has the capacity to be united with God. It is for this reason that the Franciscan theolo-gian Bonaventure described the mystery of Jesus Christ as a coincidence of opposites. Because Jesus *is* the Christ, every human is already reconciled with every other human in the mystery of the divine, so that Christ is more than Jesus alone. Christ is the whole reality bound in a union of love.

We cannot know this mystery of Christ as a doctrine or an idea; it is the root reality of all existence. Hence, we must travel inward, into the interior depth of the soul where the field of divine love is expressed in the "thisness" of our own, particular life. Each of us is a little word of the Word of God, a mini-incarnation of divine love. The journey inward requires surrender to this mystery in our lives, and this means letting go of our "control buttons." It means dying to the untethered selves that occupy us daily; it means embracing the sufferings of our lives, from the little sufferings to the big ones; it means allowing God's grace to heal us, hold us, and empower us for life; it means entering into darkness, the unknowns of our lives, and learning to trust the darkness, for the tenderness of divine love is already there; it means being willing to surrender all that we have for all that we can become in God's love; and finally, it means to let God's love heal us of the opposing tensions within us. When we can say with full voice, "You are the God of my heart, my God and my portion forever," then we can open our eyes to see that the God I seek is already in me . . . and in you. We are already One.

16.

Christ, the Future

Jesus of Nazareth was born, the world was a very different place. Local tribes formed by religious beliefs and practices marked the political scene. Jesus was born into a Jewish family descended from the tribe of Judah. He was raised according to the Torah and performed the ritual cleansings of purification. When he emerged into public ministry around the age of thirty, his provincial Middle Eastern world was rocked by political turmoil. His message was radical, inspiring, and, in many ways, startling. He had a deep awareness of God's immanent presence, and he announced to those around him that God had broken into history and was now present in their midst.

How to interpret the message of Jesus was, and still is, obscure. What did he mean by saying, "The kingdom of God is among you" (Lk 17:21) or that he must suffer and die to fulfill God's mission (Mt 16:21)? The disciples were often confused, although they loved him—except, perhaps, for Judas. They constantly wanted to be near him, to be his best friend, but Jesus was not interested in human friendships. He had one single focus—the reign of God—and he was willing to suffer and die a shameful political death so that God's reign could be realized in history.

The paradox of Jesus was that he allowed nothing to stand in the way of God's invasive love—no law, ritual, belief system, or person. When Peter identified Jesus as the Christ and became the "rock" of a new community founded on love, this "rock" of the new church was tossed into doubt and confusion when Jesus declared that he would have to suffer and die for the fulfillment of his mission. Peter was baffled and rebuked Jesus: "This must never happen to you." Peter, the rock, quickly became an obstacle to the ways of God: "Get behind me, Satan! You are a stumbling block to me; for you are setting your mind not on divine things but on human things" (Mt 16:22–23).

Jesus had a particularity of love fiercely centered on God's indwelling presence, and anything that interfered with or obscured this love was to be rejected. Yet it was this relentless particularity of love, this willingness to suffer for the sake of God, that impelled the early church to recognize Jesus as the Christ—the Anointed One. The death of an innocent man who, in the prime of his life, submitted to execution in the name of God and then rose from the dead—well, this was impossible to prove, but it was experienced by the disciples as a new power within themselves. Jesus was seen among them as a new, transformed presence. In the person of Jesus, something new broke open into history, a power like no other political or personal power, an experience of divine power that enkindled the disciples to risk their lives for the sake of the gospel. They truly believed that earthly life was opened to a new future of life in God, and that, while earthly death was integral to this new life, ultimately, they would not die.

Was Jesus really God? That was the burning question in the first few centuries of the church. By the fourth century the question of Jesus's divinity became a highly charged political debate. The priest Arius (256–366) forcefully argued that Jesus was a good man but not truly God. Athanasius (296–373) argued otherwise: If Jesus was not truly God, we are not saved. God became human so that humans could become like God. The Arian debate was fierce and widespread. Political opposition to those who defended Jesus's divinity, including Cyril of Alexandria (378–444) and Athanasius, was so volatile that Athanasius was repeatedly threatened with death and exiled five times.

The doctrine of Jesus Christ, formulated at the Council of Chalcedon in 451 CE—namely, that Jesus Christ is true God and true man—emerged out of conflicted philosophical positions and political debates. The Chalcedon formula aimed to please the two opposing christological positions, namely, the Monophysites, who emphasized one true divine nature of Christ, and the Dyophysites, who emphasized two full natures of Christ: divine and human. The conciliatory document did nothing other than appease those seeking clarity on the question of ontological natures in the person of Jesus Christ, based on Greek philosophical principles.

There is every reason to revisit the meaning of the universal Christ today, not least of which is that our understanding of nature has radically changed, thanks to modern science. We are no longer constrained within a Mediterranean basin of Greek thought, nor should we be. Jesus himself raised the question to his disciples: "Who do you say that I am?" (Mt 16:15) It was a question not to be addressed by philosophical formulas but by the experience of encounter. Many spiritual writers have said the more we enter into this question, the more it becomes a God question rather than a "self" question; we cannot adequately address the question of identity without eventually reaching the ultimate question of God. In this respect, to believe Jesus is divine and human cannot be accepted on external authority or naked faith. Rather, it must make sense on the basis of our experience: experience of self, of God, of others, and of the world.

The humanity of Jesus relates to every human person, without exception due to race, religion, language, or creed. The heart of every human person—rich, poor, black, white, Jew, or Hindu—is entangled with the spirit of God's love. Every person has a God center, every person is part of the Christ mystery, and every person can manifest the Christ. This is what Raimon Panikkar meant by the term *Christophany*. He points out that Christ is not only the name of a person in history but a reality in our own life. Christophany stands for the disclosure of Christ to human consciousness and the critical reflection upon it; each person bears the mystery of Christ within. Christ is the symbol of our human identity and vocation, which, in its acceptance and fulfillment, is the union of all created reality in the love of God.

Our first task, therefore, is to complete and perfect our icon of reality. We must enter within the cave of the human heart if we seek to know the Christ. Thomas Merton writes: "If we want to bring together what is divided . . . [then] we must contain all divided worlds in ourselves and transcend them in Christ." [1] Recognizing the inner Christ means "awakening to transcendence or spiritual reality, which initiates a personal revolution by relativizing everything that one had previously experienced or known." In the deep silence of the heart, we are opened up to a new depth of consciousness and a new relationship with this reality beyond the self.

When we awaken to the realization that the meaning of Jesus the Christ is somehow the center of reality, that our porous humanity is open to divine reality, we find that our life must be reordered to correspond to that realization. Through the human person a new reality emerges, born out of new structures of consciousness. Humanity becomes a new creative center of God's self-involving love.

---

[1] Thomas Merton, *Conjectures of a Guilty Bystander* (New York: Doubleday Image, 1968), 21.

17.

The Rainbow of Pride

For years, women and men who were not heterosexual had to hide their true identity or live secret lives. I remember when I was growing up in Totowa, New Jersey, our next-door neighbors came over to visit one evening with their two children. The man seemed uncomfortable and not all that happy and later I learned that he left his family because he was gay. My mother at the time said something to the effect, "He is a bit odd. I think he is a queer." And that is how most baby boomer and older generations viewed anyone outside the heterosexual norm. Pejorative terms were used to describe persons, as Elton John recounts in the movie *Rocketman*: "I am a fag, a puffer, a queer," terms that in the twentieth century meant, "I am an oddity, not normal." And who defined *normal*? Well, religions did a fine job limiting nature to two options, male and female, because that is how God created us, according to the book of Genesis. Yet, what we usually miss is that God created male *and* female, not male *or* female. God endowed nature with a much greater freedom of expression than humans have assumed.

One has only to study the evolution of sex from simple cellular to multicellular complex life to realize that nature is not entirely binary. The first sexual beings to emerge, perhaps 2.5 billion years ago were what biologists call isogamous—somewhere between male and female. Polygenetic types have been identified among some species, such as the cardinal and various other bird species, insects, and crustaceans. "There is a phenomenon among some birds known as bilateral gynandromorphy, where half the body is male and the other half is female, a chimera," says Daniel Hooper, a postdoctoral fellow at the Cornell Lab of Ornithology. Gynandromorphs, known as "half-siders" among ornithologists, are uncommon but not unheard of. They likely occur across all species of birds, Hooper says, but we're only likely to notice them in species where the adult males and females look distinct from each other, a trait known as sexual dimorphism.[1] As evolutionary biology unfolds, scientists are realizing there is an incredible diversity and range of genotypes among nonhuman species, leading to the remarkable revelation that nature is not clearly defined in terms of binary sexual differentiation.

Ronald Rolheiser points out that the word *sex* has a Latin root, the verb *secare*, which means "to cut off," "to sever," "to amputate," "to disconnect from the whole." To be "sexed," therefore, literally means to be cut off, to be severed from, to be amputated from the whole.[2] He uses a simple example to illustrate:

> Were you to take a chain saw and go to a tree and cut off one of its branches, you would have "sexed" that branch. This branch, could it feel and think, would wake up on the ground, severed, cut off, disconnected, a lonely little piece of wood which was once part of a great organism. It would know in its every cell that if it wants to continue living and especially if it wants to produce flowers and bear fruit, it must somehow reconnect itself to the tree.[3]

We wake up in our cribs lonely, cut off, severed from the great whole. Sex is a dimension of our very awareness, and gender is an expression of sexual identity in search of

---

[1] Maureen Seaberg, "Rare Half-Male, Half-Female Cardinal Spotted in Pennsylvania," *National Geographic*, January 31, 2019.

[2] Ronald Rolheiser, *The Holy Longing: The Search for a Christian* (New York: Doubleday, 1999), 142.

[3] Ibid., 193.

wholeness. Sexuality is a sacred energy given us by God to overcome our incompleteness, to move us toward unity and consummation with that which is beyond us. It is also the pulse to celebrate, to give and to receive delight. All of these hungers in their full maturity lead us to be fully alive as persons, co-creators with God and co-responsible with God for the planet, standing with God and blessing the world. To live chastely does not necessarily mean to live without sex but to live with the reverence of life, to experience things reverently in a way that the experience leaves both others and ourselves more integrated. We are chaste when we do not let impatience, irreverence, or selfishness ruin what is a gift by somehow violating it. When we violate anything and reduce it to an object for consumption or misuse, we violate the dignity of life and the gift of personhood.

Personhood is the heart of the matter. To be a person is to be an authentic relational being, a flowing of being in the giftedness of one's life. Personhood is not a given or a mandate; it is a constructive process of ongoing identity. To be free as persons is to be fully present to ourselves. Beatrice Bruteau writes that a person is "the creative activity of life as it projects itself to the next instant."[4] The breakthrough of personhood in recent times is a rediscovery of nature as open, porous, symbiotic, synergistic, and therefore that which cannot be bound, controlled, manipulated, or used. Rather, the fragility of boundaries and the recursive loop of identity construction means that no category can ontologically define personhood; rather, "self" is an ongoing dynamical process, a mini expanding universe open to life. This is why the rainbow aptly symbolizes the freedom and authenticity of the LGBTQ community, because it signifies the desire and hope for the fullness of life.

God looks at what God brings into being and sees it is "very good" because God is the vital core of every being, the

---

[4] Beatrice Bruteau, "The Living One," in *The Grand Option: Personal Transformation and a New Creation* (Notre Dame, IN: University of Notre Dame Press, 2001), 142.

invisible mysterious center of personhood who dwells within as fidelity in love, a love so great that every person—gay, straight, trans, bi, queer—is loved uniquely and unconditionally by God. Jesus is the symbol of the "thisness" of God. God loves *this* person, this unique gifted, blessed, individual who from all eternity is loved into beingness by the Word of God. God dwells in *this* person in no other way than the freedom of this single person.

To know God is to know oneself loved by God in the freedom of one's own self. What God desires is a heart that can respond in love: love of neighbor, love of the earth and all creatures, love of the poor, and most important, love of self. God does not know biological essentialism. God only knows the human heart, the "thisness" of you and me. We have only one real task in life: to live from the heart in truth and freedom. It is time to put away our fears and judgments and to look into the eyes of another, to gaze at the face of another, and to love the other as our self. In the words of the Sufi poet Hafiz, "[Within this gaze], I can see the Face behind every face."[5]

---

[5] Daniel Ladinsky, *A Year with Hafiz: Daily Mediations* (New York: Penguin, 2006), July 13 meditation.

18.

Race and Axial Consciousness

The question of race is so overwhelming, especially in light of current political and social fractures, that the starting point tends to be existential and anthropological. However, I wonder sometimes if the anthropological analysis is self limiting. I would like to situate race within the broader framework of axial consciousness. Our species, *Homo sapiens,* is currently thought to have originated in Africa about 140,000 years ago, eventually migrating to northern territories and spreading out. The pre-axial age marks the emergence of the tribe or the collective, which could extend as far back as the Neanderthals, to 64,000 BCE. Ancient civilizations looked at the physical and human worlds as interdependent. An imbalance in one sphere could result in an imbalance in the other. Pre-axial consciousness was a level of religious-mythic consciousness that was cosmic, collective, tribal, and ritualistic. Social and political behavior in the human sphere reflected cosmic life. Hence, cultures were intimately related to the cosmos and to the fertility cycles of nature.

While early humans were closely linked to the cosmos, they were also closely linked to one another. One gained one's identity in relation to the tribe. There was a rich and creative harmony between primal peoples and the world of nature, a harmony explored, expressed, and celebrated in myth and ritual. Myth was a way in which humans gave meaning to their world through stories, which contained essential truths. They felt themselves part of nature and experienced themselves as part of a tribe. It was precisely the web of interrelationships within the tribe that sustained them psychologically, energizing all aspects of their lives. The belief of gods or spirits in nature influenced human action and, in turn, human action (and ritual) had its effects on nature. Rituals reenacted the primordial sacrifice to maintain cosmic order and ensure the continuation of the lifecycle. Libations were performed in the home, for example, of water or fire to return these vital elements to the gods to support them, and a perpetual fire was kept burning. The sense of the whole was a sense of belonging to a web of life guided by supernatural forces or deities. All things shared the same breath of life—animals, trees, humans—all were bound together.

German philosopher Karl Jaspers coined the term *Achsenzeit* (Axial Age or Axis Age) in 1949 to describe a time between approximately 800 BCE and 200 BCE when the spiritual foundations of modern humanity were established. The axial period differed from pre-axial consciousness in that it was marked by the rise of the individual and religious cultures. The question of race begins with the rise of axial consciousness and the emergence of the human person as individual and autonomous. Modern humans are thought to have arrived in Europe from Africa around 40,000–45,000 years ago. Axial persons were in possession of their own identity, but the cost of self-identity was the loss of organic relationship to nature and community, severing the harmony with nature and the tribe.

Psychiatrist Ian McGilchrist speaks of a cognitive split in the ancient brain that can be located in the rise of the axial person. According to McGilchrist, the right brain hemisphere (the dominant hemisphere connected to the wider world) became dissociated from the left hemisphere (the analytical brain). As the lines of consciousness shifted in the axial person, from interconnected wholeness to self-reflective individuality, relationality became distorted in that connection to the wider world of nature was replaced by self-reflection and self-identity. This loss of connection to the wider cosmos had far-reaching consequences that we are experiencing today, including environmental apathy, racism, genderism, consumerism, and political factions. Jaspers suggests that this axial period amounted to "a new departure within mankind," meaning "a kind of critical, reflective questioning of the actual and a new vision of what lies beyond."[1] Jaspers and others hold that the intellectual and spiritual achievements of this time inspired most of humanity, since the foundations of all major world civilizations were laid down. He writes:

> What is new about this age . . . is that man becomes conscious of Being as a whole, of himself and his limitations. He experiences the terror of the world and his own powerlessness. He asks radical questions. Face to face with the void he strives for liberation and redemption. By consciously recognizing his limits he sets himself the highest goals. He experiences absoluteness in the depths of selfhood and in the lucidity of transcendence.[2]

William Thompson states: "What makes this period the 'axis' of human history, even our own history today, is the fact that humans emerged as 'individuals' in the proper sense."[3] Axial consciousness generated a new self-awareness, including awareness of autonomy and a new sense of individuality. The human person as *subject* emerged. The awareness

---

[1] Benjamin I. Schwartz, "The Age of Transcendence," *Daedalus* 104 (1975): 3.

[2] Karl Jaspers, "The Axial Period," in Karl Jaspers, *The Origin and Goal of History* (New Haven, CT: Yale University Press, 1953), 2. See also, S. N. Eisenstadt, ed., *The Origin and Diversity of Axial Age Civilizations*, ed. (Albany: State University of New York Press, 1986); and Karen Armstrong, in *The Great Transformation: The World in the Time of Buddha, Socrates, Confucius and Jeremiah* (London: Atlantic Books, 2006).

[3] William M. Thompson, *Christ and Consciousness: Exploring Christ's Contribution to Human Consciousness* (New York: Paulist Press, 1977), 21.

of the self in the present brought with it awareness of the self after death. People began searching for more comprehensive religious and ethical concepts, and to formulate a more enlightened morality in which each person was responsible for his or her own destiny. The sense of individual identity, distinct from the tribe and nature, is the most characteristic mark of axial consciousness. Basic to the axial period was increasing role of rationality. There were now strong communities based on intellectual assent to certain forms of behavior and/or propositions. In general, post-breakthrough societies had a greater capacity for social organization, harmony, and long-term stability.

During the Axial Age a new mode of thinking developed almost simultaneously in four major areas of the world: China, India, the Middle East, and Northern Mediterranean Europe. The world religions as we know them today emerged with a sense of divine transcendence, moral order, and longing for fulfillment. The Axial Age was a pivotal time in human history as human beings began to reflect for the first time about individual existence and the meaning of life and death. Urban civilization, initially brought about under the leadership of a priestly ruling class, encouraged trade and brought different societies closer together. But as urban life accelerated and expanded, it disrupted the old sense of order. This new way of living generated unprecedented social and political conflict and an increase in violence and aggression. People began to question their own beliefs as they came into contact with others whose beliefs were different. They were challenged to look at themselves in different ways and entertain new ideas or cling steadfastly to their old ones. People began to experience themselves as separate from others for the very first time. In this new age, Jaspers claims, "were born the fundamental categories within which we still think today; and the beginnings of the world religions, by which human beings still live, were created."[4]

---

[4] Jaspers, "The Axial Period," 2.

Anthony Black states that not all parts of the world shared in this axial breakthrough. In fact, the determining factor in the rise of organized civilization was religion. Black writes:

> Primitive societies, such as sub-Saharan Africa and pre-Columbian America, suffered severe drawbacks when they came into contact with the mentally more developed societies. They seem to have lacked, among other things, *a* sufficiently unifying set of beliefs and practices. Societies that were advanced but had no breakthrough of the kind . . . found themselves engulfed by new, more "advanced" ways of thinking; they were successively Hellenized, Christianized, Islamicized."[5]

So axial consciousness brought with it significant changes: from deep, cosmic relationality to individual introspection and self-identity; from communal, religious myth to religion of the individual in pursuit of perfection; from communal identity and cooperation to competing societies and territorial power. The difference between pre-axial and axial periods is the way religion functioned in the structures of community and power. In the axial period the Judeo-Christian tradition played a significant role in how religion gave rise to racism. Two things I want to point out here: (1) the severing of deep relationality to the cosmos eventually culminated in the metaphysical dualism of Descartes; and (2) the concept *image of God* functioned as a license for unbridled white, male power. The incarnation meant a chance to participate in God since the original Adam, created in God's image, was immortal, but lost the divine character in the fall. This was a vocation for men only. Since Eve was the root of the problem, she could not be part of the quest for perfection. To be restored in Adam was a male endeavor, and it meant to have dominion over nature, which translated into white, male power ruling over nonwhites, women and nature itself.

---

[5] Anthony Black, "The Axial Period: What Was It and What Does It Signify?" *Review of Politics* 70/1 (2008): 38–39.

A closed-system mentality of clericalism was built into the Adam myth. Whether or not one was ordained, the divine right to power was pervasive. Failing to achieve divine perfection drove the white European male to conquer and divide at all costs. Severed from the wider cosmic community, the white male felt empowered by God to be Godlike or risk death and nothingness. If axial consciousness gave birth to the human person as individual, the religious trajectory of axial consciousness unraveled the human person as relational. Axial individualism, the difference of color (and gender), and the quest for God power all fueled the unbelievable horror and tragedies of racism and genderism. The Enlightenment consolidated power in the white European male. The death of God and the rise of Nietzsche's *übermensch* ("superman") meant the final blow to the relational human. Race and gender became determining factors of who counts as a human person and who does not.

This religious trajectory of axial consciousness became so distorted with regard to race that J. Kameron Carter's expression, the "politics of melanin," is pivotal. If we follow the evolutionary trajectory, the human race began with dark skin and eventually lightened with migration to northern climates, that is, away from the equatorial sun. So the human species began rich in melanin, which eventually diminished with less sun and colder climates. The politics of melanin is both fascinating and frightening.

The early twenty-first century is experiencing the final phases on racism and genderism that emerged in the axial period. The advent of computer technology and the internet have rapidly shifted the lines of human consciousness away from individualism toward hyper-personalization. We are at the beginning of second axial consciousness and posthuman life. In the second axial period personhood is being liberated from individualism as new types of relationality emerge. The first axial individual is coming to an end and giving way to the second axial person, as lines of consciousness shift from the vertical individualism to the horizontal and globalized hyper-connected person. The second axial person is best described as *posthuman,* a term that signifies the end of the liberal subject modeled on the white European male. The posthuman is not readily identified because there are no real physical changes. Biological diversity belonged to evolution's expanding phase, which is now over. What is changing is the level of human consciousness in relation to the environment, and this shift of consciousness reflects the need to overcome ontologically defined boundaries.

The new person emerging in evolution does not differ physically but mentally, that is, by the way he or she thinks about the world and about his or her body in the world. The posthuman of the second axial period has a new electronically embedded body with an electronically embedded mind. Ontologies are becoming redefined because meaningful existence now emerges in the "splices," that is, the spaces in-between where coded information complexifies. The post-human is increasingly gender fluid, racially neutral and inter-spiritual. The fluidity of boundaries and the recursive loop of ongoing identity construction means that no category can adequately define personhood. Rather, the "self" is an ongoing discovery and creative process of belonging to the whole. Beatrice Bruteau writes: "The more conscious the individual becomes, the more the individual becomes *person,* and each person is person only to the extent that the individual freely lives by the life of the Whole."[6]

The emerging posthuman is a new type of person wired toward engagement, communication, and shared information. Gen Y and Gen Z populations, in particular, are oriented toward posthuman life marked by shared being and a deep concern for the earth community. Growing up in a networked world means that personhood is a cybernetic process, an ongoing process that embraces pluralities of gender, race, and religion. Self-identity is self-creative through self-

---

[6] Beatrice Bruteau, "The Whole World: A Convergent Perspective," in *The Grand Option* (Notre Dame, IN: University of Notre Dame Press, 2001), 102.

engagement. What constitutes the "self" is the dynamic and ineffable core constitutive relationship, which is always a particularity in movement, so that personhood is performative; the art of becoming person is a creative act. The body-world relationship is the creative process of self-identity so that purity of skin color does not depend on melanin but on authenticity, transparency, and expressiveness. In this respect, various skin colors may be complexified with colored tattoos, colored hair, and colored nails. Color is no longer an ontological distinction but a hyper-personal expression of shared being. In this hyper-connected, hyper-personalized sphere, interbeing supersedes individual being so that interracial relations, and interreligious relations, intergender relations are all part of the normative, creative act of personal identity. To put this another way, the mixture of races, genders, and religions is no longer the exception but the norm. We are creating a world of deep relationality because we are being rewired for belonging to the cosmic whole, suggested by the term *global consciousness*. The question of race is a question of personal identity, and a networked world is shifting the boundaries of personhood and identity.

A number of years ago, I was teaching Franciscan theology in England and had a group of African Sisters from Nigeria in class. At the final class I asked the students to say a few words on what was meaningful for them in the course. One robust African sister in full habit got up and walked to the front of the class and said, "You have spoken deeply to my heart, and I shall never forget this class." Then she broke into song and the other African sisters joined in. For a moment the entire classroom was lifted up into the most beautiful, magical moment of love; there was a palpable unity in our midst. No longer were we white or black or American or European or African—we were one heart united in the song that burst forth from a heart full of love, a *human* heart in which every person resonated like a string attuned to the harmony of love.

We should never forget the enormous sufferings that the politics of melanin have caused, but at the same we need to grasp the reins of our present forces of evolution and co-create a new world bounded in love.

Sext

The Spirit blows where it wills.
Does the Spirit actually "blow" like wind?
Could something that "blows" like wind
Have a will?
Just think or imagine for a second,
The Spirit is not
Something
But *Someone*-in-Between.
The Metaxological person,
The Personal center of Betweenness.
Neither "this" nor "that"
But "this" and "that"
After all, how could any "thing" relate
If it was not first relatable?
The Spirit is the relatable person.
Which means, of course, that we are first
Spirit, since it is first "we" then "me."
Which means we are first "this and that," depth and
breadth,
somewhere in-between, and then
I exist.
Which means of course that this blowing Spirit
Is no willy-nilly
There is a mysterious center of attraction
To this unfathomable depth
Turning this relatable in-between

Energy of life into
My life.
The Spirit is Love-
Breathing life, and my life is
Life-breathing Love.
Which is why matter can never be lonely,
Gravity is matter's response
to loneliness;
the Spirit dances in quarks.
And Love pulls the whole
into God.

19.

The Core Energy of Love

ow do we know if our thinking and doing is coming
from the ground of love? We know love implicitly
because we feel love as a deepening of well-being in relation to another—whether a friend, partner, spouse, or God.
Love brings a sense of joy, peace, wholeness, and belonging.
Without love we experience emptiness, loneliness, or abandonment, a deep thirst, so to speak, as if in a vast desert.
Love can be defined as the good within me that attends to
the good in you. By *good* I mean that which is wholesome,
positive, life-giving being. Because I experience these qualities in a particular way within me and in a different way in
you, and because what I experience in you is different from
me, I am attracted to you precisely because you help complete what is lacking in me. Hence, I love you as the other
as part of myself because you help complete me. Love draws
together and unites, and in uniting, one to the other, it differentiates. I am more myself together in union with another
than when I am alone or cut off from others. In this way love
fills the deepest center of my heart because the need to belong to another ultimately expresses my need for God. In the
words of Saint Augustine: "You have made us for yourself,
O Lord, and our hearts are restless until they rest in you."

If I were truly my own maker, I would have no existential
need for anyone else and thus no need for love. I am created by God, and this alone means I have an intrinsically
relational self that can only find its fulfillment in God—and
where God lives—in my heart and in the heart of every

person I meet. But the fulfillment of love does not come easily, because my ego is often contracted and closed in on itself, and thus I must continuously strive to grow into God. Bernard of Clairvaux sees conversion as the path to love and spoke of the four stages of love. On the first level, he says, we love ourselves; on the second level we love God for ourselves; on the third level we love ourselves for the sake of God; and on the fourth level we love God for the sake of the God. He writes that *God* is the reason for loving God. And to love totally is the way to love God. On this highest level of love we love completely with no thought of self, because the self lives entirely in, with, and for God. This highest stage of love is selfless love because in giving myself completely to God and to the other in whom God lives I find my joy. Bonaventure spoke of highest level of selfless love as a "death" insofar as the ego disappears and God becomes the living center of the heart.

Pierre Teilhard de Chardin speaks of love as the core energy of the universe, the primal blood flow of the universe. As entities attract and unite, something new is created. Because of these energies, the universe orients itself toward intelligent, conscious, self-reflective life.

For Teilhard, love is a passionate force at the heart of the Big Bang universe, the fire that breathes life into matter and unifies elements center to center; love is a cosmological force. He writes: "Love is the most universal, the most tremendous and the most mysterious of the cosmic forces. . . . The physical structure of the universe is love." [1] Love-energy is the history of the universe, present from the Big Bang onward, though indistinguishable from molecular forces. "But even among the molecules, love was the building power that worked against entropy, and under its attraction the elements groped their way toward union." [2] Love draws

---

[1] Pierre Teilhard de Chardin, *Human Energy*, trans. J. M. Cohen (New York: Harcourt Brace Jovanovich, 1969), 72.

[2] Ibid., 33.

together and unites; in uniting, it differentiates. Love-energy is intrinsically relational and undergirds relationality in the universe. Union is the end toward which each being directs itself. Love is the affinity of being with being in a personal, centered way, a unity toward more being that marks all cosmic life. If there was no internal propensity to unite, even at a rudimentary level, Teilhard writes, indeed in the molecule itself—it would be physically impossible for love to appear higher up, in a hominized form. Cosmic life is intrinsically communal. The universe is thoroughly relational and in the framework of love.

Love, therefore, is an absolute fundamental force of attraction in the universe that overcomes all inertia, entropy, breakdown, and dissipation. It is a unitive energy that can draw life out of a black hole, a region of space-time from which nothing can escape it—except perhaps the absolute power of love, which is God-Omega. For this reason Teilhard sees cosmic evolution as a process of amorization, love-energy is building up in the universe through center-to-center attraction, because God is rising up in the universe, eventually arriving at a level of self-conscious love, the human level where we must choose to love. For as we grow into love, we grow into freedom and thus we ultimately must make a choice to love or to reject love. For God to live, we must choose to love. Teilhard writes:

> Love alone is capable of completing our beings in themselves as it unites them, for the good reason that love alone takes them and joins them by their very depths. . . . All around us at every moment does love not accomplish that magic act . . . of personalizing as it totalizes? And if it does this on a daily basis on a reduced scale, why could it not someday repeat it in the dimensions of the earth?[3]

---

[3] Pierre Teilhard de Chardin, *The Phenomenon of Man*, trans. Bernard Wall (New York: Harper and Row, 1959), 189.

It is love that draws this world onward toward greater personal unity in which God is revealed. But we must constantly work against the power of the ego to contract on itself, isolating us from the unitive power of love—which is why the grace of God is essential (attending to the Omega center within) if we are to transcend our partial loves toward a greater wholeness. Only one who is absolute being in love can draw us beyond contracted selves toward the fullness of love—and this is God-Omega, who is within and ahead.

If we are to reveal, to understand, to listen and attend, to celebrate, to be with others, then love must ultimately live in an ongoing spirit of forgiveness, recognizing that each of us is a partial whole, a bit broken, somewhat in darkness, uncomfortable with our incomplete life, and so we are all yearning to belong to the One who can make us whole and fulfill the deepest longings of our heart. To forgive one another is to let go of past hurts in order to create a new future together, for love always lives on the horizon of the future.

Love, in a sense, is always moving out of a black hole of nothingness into the bright light of a future fullness. It is an ongoing creative process, an amorizing of relationships through the outward flow of goodness and the receptivity of being. We humans are not doing too well at it, and we are missing out on the core energy of our lives. But the stars learned to forgive long ago, so too did the mountains and the valleys, the giraffe seahorses, the lemon trees, and the weeping willows. All of nature lives in the spirit of forgiveness because nature lives in the beauty of love. We must learn to love over and over again if we are to evolve into a unified planet, a wholeness of being, an earth community of compassion and peace. How shall we do so in this complex world? Saint John of the Cross advises us to put love where there is no love, and then we will find love.

20.

The Power of Faith

ears ago I lived with a sister in New Jersey who constantly complained about being overlooked in the community. One day she was on a tirade about a position in the nursing home that had been given to another sister who, in her view, was less qualified for the job. After listening for several minutes to her rant, I quietly said, "Well, why don't you go and talk to her, and maybe you can work something out?" "Oh," she responded, "she has been dead for ten years!" Some people walk around with dead bones in their bodies and cannot shake the dust from their feet. If nature held on to the many conflicts and deaths that took place over billions of years, we would not be here. Instead, nature has a built-in sense of letting go when life gets stifled."

In *Capture: Unraveling the Mystery of Mental Suffering*, David A. Kessler, MD, describes how the mind can imprison memories by locking the information into a repetitive circuit. We humans are so mysteriously bound together that we are unaware at times of how the mind can capture an idea or an event and spin it around in the circuits of our brain, like a spider's web, until the brain captures the idea and holds the mind prisoner.[1] Prayer and meditation can help unravel this mental grip, but only if the will is oriented toward God or something outside ourselves that is drawing us to more life.

---

[1] David A. Kessler, MD, *Capture: Unraveling the Mystery of Mental Suffering* (New York: Harper Wave, 2016).

Jesuit priest Walter Ciszek was sentenced to twenty-three years of hard labor in Siberia following five years in solitary confinement at Lubyanka prison on the charge that he was a Vatican spy. In *With God in Russia* he recounts feeling bitter and abandoned by God, but he notes that he continued to pray even when it seemed that God had abandoned him. In his second book, *He Leadeth Me,* he describes his journey from spiritual desolation to spiritual consolation as he surrendered to the will of God. It was a radical decision in the face of a dire predicament. Either God was real and the ground of his life, or God did not exist.

> There was but a single vision, God, who was all in all; there was but one will that directed all things, God's will. I had only to see it, to discern it in every circumstance in which I found myself and let myself be ruled by it. God is in all things, sustains all things, directs all things. To discern this in every situation and circumstance, to see His will in all things, was to accept each circumstance and situation and let oneself be borne along in perfect confidence and trust. Nothing could separate me from Him, because He was in all things. No danger could threaten me, no fear could shake me, except the fear of losing sight of Him. The future, hidden as it was, was hidden in His will and therefore acceptable to me no matter what it might bring. The past, with all its failures, was not forgotten; it remained to remind me of the weakness of human nature and the folly of putting any faith in self. But it no longer depressed me. I looked no longer to self to guide me, relied on it no longer in any way, so it could not again fail me. By renouncing, finally and completely, all control of my life and future destiny, I was relieved as a consequence of all responsibility. I was freed thereby from anxiety and worry, from every tension, and could float serenely upon the tide of God's sustaining providence in perfect peace of soul.[2]

---

[2] Walter Ciszek, SJ, *He Leadeth Me: An Extraordinary Testament of Faith* (New York: Doubleday, 1973), 79–80.

This testimony of faith is remarkable. At some point we have to decide to either live in the illusion of the past or to surrender to God, who is the power of the future.

To let go of the past is to be free of the emotional constraints captured by the mind. Such letting go is possible if there is a greater force—God—pulling us ahead. We may not be able to forget the past but we can *forgive* wrongdoing if we trust that we are loved by a power greater than ourselves. Surrender to this power means loving in the present moment and openness to future life. We love not to correct the past but to create a new future. Forgiveness is an act of creative freedom and is radically novel when we give out of an abundance of goodness for the sake of a new future. We evolve to never stop evolving—this is the deepest truth of our reality. Life begins anew each time we love because God is ever newness in love. To let go and surrender to the creative will of God is to be part of the dynamism of divine love, forever participating in the newness of life unto the greater fullness of life. For this reason, as Beatrice Bruteau writes, "creativity may be the real interior meaning of the act of faith."[3]

---

[3] Beatrice Bruteau, *The Grand Option: Personal Transformation and a New Creation* (Notre Dame, IN: University of Notre Dame Press, 2001), 172.

21.

Fire Burns and So Does Love

We live today between power and defeat, and as a result, there is a lot of mental and emotional fatigue. Greta Thunberg, the young prophet of climate change, in January 2020 spoke at the economic forum in Davos, Switzerland, saying that, with regard to carbon emissions, nothing has changed. Recent devastating fires in Australia and California are signs that global warming can induce dramatic consequences, and yet even these destructive fires are swept off the map of consumer culture as another algorithm crossing our computer screens. The typical Facebook response is "prayers needed." In the face of unbridled and corrupt political power, our sense of freedom is being crushed by a rising feeling of despair.

And yet, if I ascend in an airplane to thirty thousand feet, I get a very different view of things from what *Time* magazine or the *Economist* reports. Pulling away and rising above the clamor of competing forces, I see a majestic beauty of rolling fields and mountains as I sail through clouds. It is truly amazing that the human person can imagine, create, and build an airplane that transports and transcends, and yet, at the same time, the human person can lie, cheat, corrupt, maim, and destroy. What are we humans anyway? This is the great question of every century. In the past, religions told us what we were: creatures in the image of God, noble centers of creation endowed with reason and immortal souls. Today, technology tries to claim that position, indicating that we are downloadable software in replaceable hardware. Technology has our attention, but religion is what we long for—not the old stuff but a new religious spirit, a harnessing of our energies toward ultimate meaning that binds us to ultimate life, living with purpose not just for ourselves but for the whole cosmic life, which we implicitly know we belong to.

For millions of years biological life fashioned for itself different tools and arrangements that enabled the flourishing of life, for example, the construction of clam shells, the burrowing of fox holes, the construction of beaver dams, and a myriad of other "technologies" to safeguard and optimize biological life. Many people think that biology and technology are opposites, with the former being "natural" while the other is "manmade." Nothing could be further from the truth. Technology is not a human invention; it is an essential aspect of nature by which life seeks the means and tools to orient itself toward more life. Yes, humans are clever, but so too is nonhuman nature; rather, we are clever because nature is clever. Given our long biological history, it is fair to say that nature itself may be cleverer than humans. We boast of our superior intelligence, but our higher cognitive skills come at a high price. We can blindly choose against nature, and choosing against nature can create artificial constructs that have little to do with nature. Today we are experiencing artificial religion, artificial politics, and artificial socialization—all these systems function outside the principles of nature. These systems are no longer consonant with nature, as science now describes it. These artificial systems are more artificial than artificial intelligence (AI), which really is not artificial at all, but rather an extension of our biological intelligence. What is interesting is why we are building AI in the first place. To be human is to imagine what does not exist and to create what we imagine. AI expresses our collective imagination; it is a mirror of our deepest desires, and what we desire is to get out of *here* and be *there*. *There* is anywhere but *here*. This sounds very much like Plato's cave, and, in truth, we have not strayed too far from the Greek philosopher. Maybe it is because we want to be anywhere but here that we have neglected the earth.

Yet nature itself does not dream. It deals with reality and presses on. In a recent article on the fires in the Australia, one survivor said that his backyard was a wasteland of dead wood, charred trees stripped bare in a graveyard of ashes. However, he said, he went out one day to look more closely at the dead wood and found that some of the trees had tiny buds of new life. Life presses through dead wood and stretches toward new life. Theologians want to jump on this right away and say that new buds formed because God is in the tree. And yet, such a statement really undermines the tree, as if, well, maybe it only appeared to burn up or God let it burn so that God could save it. The more I think how out of touch theology is with nature, the more I am on the side of the dead tree and the ability of the dead tree to be dead and alive at the same time.

The truth is, matter is really strange stuff. Einstein's theory of special relativity took a sledgehammer to Aristotle and his disciples; matter is not substance, and energy is not a relation. That matter and energy are interconvertible facts puts the stuff of reality on a whole new level of knowledge whereby experience and observation play a fundamental role. David Bohm's implicate order, a theory Einstein was not too fond of, comes close to a twentieth-century Neoplatonic revival whereby the One is in the many and yet transcends the many, or, as Alfred North Whitehead put it, the many become one and are increased by one.

Whereas theologians should probably throw Einstein a party every year or celebrate Herbert Minkowski as the saint of quantum physics, theologians are like aliens on earth when it comes to modern science. They might feel better if they could realize that scientists are themselves baffled and confused by the implications of quantum physics. The well-worn scientific method simply does not hold up to nature's weirdness. Philosophers are pointing out that consciousness is now a problem, because without consciousness there is simply no science, and yet no one really knows what consciousness is. The inability of quantum reality to be reduced to quantifiable measurements of ontological certainty is problematic. As a result, there are conflicting schools of thought, and science spills over into philosophy, and philosophy "cherry picks" the scientific data to create new theories. And who knows where the theologians are, because if they showed up in this chaotic conversation there might be some resolve between science and philosophy. But, alas, very few theologians have been noted at this party, and those who do show up are deemed heretics or are simply ignored.

Given this state of affairs among the key pillars of human knowledge, it is no wonder that oligarchs and demagogues have rushed in to fill the gaps created by academics wrapped up in their highly sophisticated paradigms. To put this another way, the university is no longer a help but a hindrance to our entropic world. And yet, reflecting on this chaos from thirty thousand feet, there is something else going on, something deeper and more hopeful. Chaos theory, formulated by meteorologist Edward Lorenz in the 1960s, basically states that in open systems, a spontaneous basin of attraction can emerge and pull a system into a new pattern of order over time. Biological evolution gives witness to life as a series of interweaving open systems. Things break down and die, but death releases nutrients and resources for new life; breakdown is a new level of breakthrough. Life is open to more life. The key to chaos theory is to focus not so much on the breakdown of order but on the *strange attractor,* the basin of attraction within the system yet different from the system. Paying close attention to the new basin of attraction leads to recognition of a fractal, a new pattern of order emerging from the decaying system. Fractals repeat themselves over time until a new pattern becomes visible. Life celebrates itself with novel order. What are the strange attractors in our midst?

With all our energy spent on political survival and global warming, what are we missing? From thirty thousand feet one of the most remarkable attractors is the shrinking of the globe due to information networks and global travel. We are more and more one earth community. We have our differences in culture, language, politics, and so on, but underneath these differences there is a consciousness of belonging to the whole planet. Younger generations, especially Gen Z, know this wholeness intuitively, and there is deep concern for the welfare of the planet and the poor. In my view this new planetary consciousness flows from the way information and cybernetics have reorganized human personhood. Youth are born into a networked world and think across lines of relationship; they are born for a new wholeness and, in a sense, a new catholicity.

With the new insights from systems biology, quantum physics, and consciousness studies, and the emerging philosophies grappling with the new data, the one discipline needed to bring this budding new fractal into a meaningful framework of purpose and aim is theology. It is not enough to talk about finding God in the stars or the cosmic Christ or that one God creates one creation and we are all brothers and sisters. These are all abstractions based on a confluence of scripture, medieval theology, and some philosophical ideas thanks to Kant, Hegel, and Heidegger. Despite the many efforts to rework ethics and spirituality for a world of cultural, religious, and social pluralism, such efforts, without dealing with the stuff of matter itself, are untethered and flimsy, intellectual teasers in need of a theological vision. They may do some good, but they cannot bring about the long overdue shift needed for a world in evolution, that is, the God shift. Fundamental theology (even the name itself connotes another era) must come to the party where science and philosophy are sitting at the table. Some twentieth-century theologians, like Karl Rahner, understood this need but did not sufficiently engage the sciences.

Most theologians want to keep dead thinkers alive out of reverential nostalgia because there is no real grasp of evolution. But in evolution nothing is ever lost; rather, things are subsumed or taken up into the new so that the seeds of the old give birth to the new and become new themselves in the process. Evolution is not linear, nor does it follow Pythagorean geometry. Rather, it is a complex process of open dynamical systems in which quantum physics, information, and cybernetics undergird interdependent systems. Most theologians do not know what to do with evolution, so they ignore it. In his own way Pope Francis understands the significance of the sciences for theology. Anyone who has faith in God without faith in the world and, in particular, the world of matter, does not have faith in a *living* God.

The ancients knew that if God is Creator, then creation reflects God. Yet we have done our best, especially in institutional religion, to skirt around the mirror of creation. A mirror reflects what is visible, and the mirror of creation is a mirror of quantum strangeness, or better yet, quantum mystery, a mirror of matter-spirit-consciousness completely entangled. Without looking into the mirror of creation, we cannot see the face of God.

We can certainly meditate and refocus our energies, but without engaging the mysterious stuff of life in all its weirdness, our prayers can redound on hyper-individualism. We live in an open-systems world, a world of losses and gains, spontaneity and creativity, appearances and disappearances. It is precisely the weirdness of nature that undergirds its radical interconnectivity. Unless we are at home in a world of ever-moving relationships, entangled knots of conscious matter, then we are not at home in a world with a future, because the future is the sign of a strange and unpredictable reality.

We are and should be concerned about global warming and the fires destroying homes and fields. But we should be more concerned about the lack of fire in the church, a fire needed to update the core truths of theology. "I came to bring fire to the earth," Jesus said, "and how I wish it were already kindled" (Lk 12:49). We have lost the passion of Jesus to challenge the boundaries of established laws and doctrines. We do not have the courage to turn over the altar to women, to stand before bishops and priests with assurance that God is doing new things, that women can fully participate in the church as priests and deacons and God will not mind one bit. We do not have the passion to be creative and imaginative, to envision a new church and a new collaboration of religions in the world. We stick with the old, as if religion is immutable, the great exception to evolution. Yet science tells us that nature has the capacity to do new things. God is perfectly at home with the strange relationships of quantum reality and evolution.

After 13.8 billion years of cosmic life and 4.2 billion years of earth life, nature has shown itself resilient in the face of destruction. This resilience bears witness to the hope that life will win the race. Theology should give voice to this hope and not stifle it by outdated otherworldly doctrines and rituals. There is a desperate need for an earthy God, one who is at home in messy nature. Science can only bring us so far; in the end, it will disappoint us. It is Love that meets the needs of the human heart and binds together in a unity that grows. The best name for God is Love.

22.

The Ineffable Bond of Love

As I prepare to teach my final classes this week, I am grateful for the development of computer technology and its ability to facilitate personal communication. Without the internet and online platforms such as Zoom, during times such as the pandemic shutdown we would be completely isolated from one another, and education would be left entirely up to parents. Yet, here we are, able to share insights, teach lessons, and learn without leaving our rooms. We can thank Alan Turing, Steve Jobs, Bill Gates, and the pioneers of computer technology who brilliantly created the devices that now save us from pandemic isolation. One of my students wisely suggested that we have grown so accustomed to internet connectivity that we feel deeply alienated with social distancing. He wrote: "Smartphones and laptops have altered the way we perceive what it means to be human, and maybe this quarantine seems more extreme than it would have seemed twenty years ago because we are more connected than ever."

While technology is extremely helpful, it cannot replace the infinite value of human relationships. I wonder if we invented computer technology in the first place because we have an intrinsic need for human relationships. We long to be accepted and loved, to share life with another person. After all, computer technology emerged after we blew up Europe and watched thousands of innocent people suffer exile and death in concentration camps. If this pandemic has done anything positive for us, it has made us rethink what it means to be human.

Computer technology, on the other hand, has made consumerism into a god, an absolute horizon of desire where more is better and better is the road to happiness. But the more we run after stuff, the more we forget where stuff comes from; hence, we forget the earth, the poor, natural resources, sweat shops, child labor, and the chain of consumer goods, all of which are invisible to the lures of marketing. The Western world built itself on the Weberian idea of hard work, thrift, savings, and accumulation. For Max Weber and the spirit of capitalism, wealth accumulated by hard work—"just wealth"—receives the blessing of God and the reward of eternal happiness: "Blessed are those who work and become wealthy for theirs is the kingdom of heaven." But if heaven is the openness of earth to its fulfillment in the God, can heaven be attained only by hard-working, wealthy individuals? I do not think so. God chose to be with the *anawim*, the poor ones, because those who are poor are in need of others. Heaven is what we become in love: shared life. The fullness of shared life on earth will be the absolute joy of heaven.

The COVID-19 virus has unsettled the relationship between technology and consumerism, and we are not sure what this will mean for us. But it may invite us to slow down and consider the infinite value of human relationships. Did you ever sit with a friend and share a meal, or a drink, and experience an ineffable bond, a quality of relationship that cannot be adequately described because words cannot grasp the depth of the space in-between, which is no longer space but a living flame of love? I remember one time being with a good friend. We were just hanging out, not doing much, just talking about the little things of life. Yet, in that moment I was conscious of an ineffable "being with," a belonging, in such a way that I thought, "This must be what heaven is like." In that moment I had the experience of joy, peace, and true happiness.

Such moments are the precious bonds of human relationships. They cannot be bought or sold; they can take place in large mansions or small huts. They emerge, often spontane-ously, from a deep goodness that flows from one person to another. We can name this ineffable bond of love as God's Spirit, for indeed where two or more are gathered in the openness of shared life, there is God.

In the end, the only thing that will matter will be how well we loved. If the pandemic has taught us anything, it is to pay attention to the person we encounter, more so, to be attentive to the ones we love (and often take for granted). To be present in the moment, heart and soul, attentive to the sounds of life in the midst of anxiety, laughter, sorrow, and wonder. Heaven opens where we are and invites us in as we are. The moral of the story is that grace is everywhere and love abounds, but it must be received and celebrated. This is the sacrament of everyday life.

None

Though frightened for a moment by evolution,
the Christian now perceives that what it offers him is
nothing
but a magnificent means of feeling more at one with God
and of giving himself more to him.
In a pluralistic and static Nature,
the universal domination of Christ could,
strictly speaking,
still be regarded as an extrinsic
and super-imposed power.
In a spiritually converging world
this "Christic" energy
acquires an urgency and
intensity of another order altogether. . . .
Christ invests himself organically
with the very majesty of his creation.
And it is in no way metaphorical
to say
that man finds himself
capable of experiencing
and discovering his God
in the whole length,
breadth and depth of the world
in movement.
To be able to say literally
to God

that one loves him,
not only with all one's body,
all one's heart and
all one's soul,
but with every fibre
of the unifying universe—
that is a prayer
that can only be made
in space-time.[1]

---

[1] Pierre Teilhard de Chardin, *The Phenomenon of Man*, trans. Bernard Wall (New York: Harper and Row, 1959), 297.

23.

Despite the News,
We Belong to One Another

$\mathcal{M}$odern science has revealed new information about the human person. If we drill down to the depths of nature, we see that we are wholes within wholes communicating information across complex fields of energy. Physicist David Bohm speaks of fundamental reality as an implicate order that has endless depth and movement: "As humans and societies we seem separate but in our roots we are part of an indivisible whole and share in the same cosmic process."[1] On higher-ordered levels of nature we are beginning to see that systems in nature do not work on principles of competition and struggle but on cooperation and sympathy. Peter Wohlleben's book *The Hidden Life of Trees* is a radical disclosure of nature's social justice. Wohlleben, a forester by training, found a tree that had been cut down centuries ago was still alive. How was this possible since without leaves, a tree is unable to perform photosynthesis, which is how it converts sunlight into sugar for sustenance? The ancient tree was clearly receiving nutrients in some other way—for hundreds of years. What scientists have found, Wohlleben writes, is that neighboring trees help one another through their root systems—either directly, by intertwining their roots, or indirectly, by growing fungal networks around the roots that serve as a sort of extended nervous system connecting separate trees.

---

[1] David Bohm, *Wholeness and the Implicate Order* (New York: Routledge and Kegan Paul, 1980), 5.

Wohlleben pondered this astonishing sociality of trees and wondered about what makes strong human communities and societies. Why are trees such social beings? Why do they share food with their own species and sometimes even go so far as to nourish their competitors? The reasons are the same as for human communities: there are advantages to working together. American forest ecologist Suzanne Simard found that primeval forests, that is, "natural" forests undisturbed by man as opposed to "plantation" forests managed for commercial benefit, have a layer of fungus called mycelium under the topsoil, which connects individual trees. other. This layer forms a kind of dense "social" network that *Nature* magazine dubbed the "wood wide web." Trees use this layer to exchange nutrients and food, to "support" those sick or weak and to "inform" each other of threats.

The hidden communal life of trees is reflective of nature's wholeness. What we can say, broadly speaking, is that nature is a communion of subjects functioning on principles of wholeness that include mutual cooperation, sympathy, and synergy. In distinction to the natural world, humans have become individual consumers, self-absorbed individuals who relate to one another as foreign objects. Nature works along lines of cooperation and organization, while humans work individually, according to principles of competition and power. Nature is like a weaver, constantly threading together the myriad layers of energy fields, whereas humans are like individual atoms bumping into one another. Biological nature lives in harmony with the cosmos, whereas humans have come to live "acosmically."

Refocusing God and World

Teilhard de Chardin realized that the gap between science and religion lies at the core of our systemic dysfunction. Religion has become fossilized, while science has discovered an entirely new universe. Nature reveals a luminous thread of justice coursing throughout its systems, while religion sputters around on a circular road, like moss in a stagnant pond. Teilhard struggled to redefine Christianity as a religion of evolution. Despite the long history of the universe, evolution continues in a direction of increasing complexity, suggesting a force in nature that resists entropy and empowers newness. Teilhard named this energizing principle of wholeness as Omega and identified Omega with God. God is not found through opposition to matter (anti-matter) or independent of matter (extra-matter) but through matter (trans-matter). We take hold of God in the finite; God is rising or emerging from the depths of matter, born not in the heart of matter but *as* the heart of matter.

Teilhard was concerned with the evolution of justice. Rather than positing an idealism of the common good, he realized that the heart of matter is consciousness, which expresses itself in love-energy. God is entangled with nature in a way that divine consciousness seeks to raise unconscious matter to new levels of consciousness and thus new levels of love. Our task is to wake up to the truth of our reality (by *truth* Teilhard means that which glues life together and renders it fecund). This waking up requires interiority and centeredness. Hence, the first step toward justice is focusing the mind on higher-ordered levels of love. Life in evolution requires living inward and moving outward, that is, living from an inner unified space of conscious awareness and presence whereby we see the divine light shining through every aspect of our world—even the ugly parts—because nothing is outside the embrace of God's love. Life in evolution means that we are moving, we are becoming something new, not just individually but collectively because we are unfinished and God is doing new things.

Faith in the World

To participate in the world's becoming we must have faith in one another and faith in the world. This is what it means to have faith in God. As early as 1916 Teilhard wrote: "There is a communion with God, and a communion with earth, and a communion with God through earth."[2] Human beings complete themselves in the higher consciousness that is part of the evolving process of formation. What constitutes the "good" is everything that brings a growth of consciousness to the world. What is best is what assures the highest development of consciousness and thus the spiritual growth of the earth. A new morality of growth is one that will foster and catalyze evolutionary change, a growth into a new formation of being, a deepening of what we are together in which care for another humanizes us. In Teilhard's view, religion should empower the evolutionary process by inspiring us to take responsibility for the earth and for the future and the evolutionary process itself. In this respect religion must be primarily *on the level of human consciousness* and human action rather than in institutions or belief systems, except insofar as these manifest and give direction to the former. A rightly understood faith in the future and the idea of a possible awakening of a higher state of consciousness are both seen as necessary for preserving in human beings the taste for action.

Teilhard's vision of a new religion of the earth means that individual spirituality is no longer enough. Religions need to recalibrate their vital centers with the cosmos. We need to find a way to harness the mystical currents of the established religious traditions and refocus them on gathering the human community into a common spiritual center so that cooperation and working together for the future may be enkindled. Teilhard spoke of an ethics oriented toward the future, which means nurturing the values that gather us in, bond us together, create a global consciousness and a cosmic heart. These values are not fixed; rather, *they must be continuously discovered and discerned*. The future is our reality; it is our common good. We are responsible for the future. Integral to this emerging future is the development of personhood and

---

[2] Pierre Teilhard de Chardin, *Writings in Time of War*, trans. René Hague (New York: William Collins Sons and Co., 1968), 14.

self-actualization. Justice is the work of humanization and personalization, and therefore it is mutual in nature. In the words of Beatrice Bruteau: "We cannot wait for the world to turn, for the times to change that we may change with them. . . .We ourselves *are* the future and we *are* the revolution. If and when the next revolution comes, it will come as we turn and the world turns with us."[3] Bruteau, like Teilhard, realized that we can only build the world together if we are becoming persons together.

---

[3] Beatrice Bruteau, "Neofeminism and the Next Revolution in Consciousness," *Cross Currents* (Summer 1977): 182.

24.

Praying in Teilhard's Universe

$\mathcal{T}$homas of Celano, the first biographer of Saint Francis of Assisi, wrote that Francis did not so much pray as he became a living prayer. I think the same could be said of Teilhard de Chardin. What does it mean to be a person of living prayer? And how does such a person live in an unfinished universe? First of all, prayer is my awakening to the fact that I am held in being by God, who is the source of my life, the divine ground of my life, who is other than me yet at the heart of me. Prayer is God's breathing in me by which I become part of the intimacy of God's inner life and God becomes the active living presence of my life. A person of living prayer lives from a deep wellspring of God-centeredness in such a way that, through prayer, God and self are continuously born into a new existence, a new person in Christ.

Teilhard, like Francis of Assisi, was a man steeped in prayer, whereby his mind expanded into a cosmotheandric solidarity, a oneness with God that flowed from a deep mesh of energies at the core of his life. Through prayer, Teilhard became a stranger to the human sphere of competition, greed, and individualism and found his humanity at home in the cosmos; that is to say, Teilhard found the truth of his life in the world of matter, the world of physical reality, and hence the world of experience.

In "The Spiritual Power of Matter" Teilhard wrote in a lyrical and mystical way of the power of matter in which divinity is hidden. Building on the spiritual stages of purgation,

illumination, and union, he describes an asceticism of surrender to matter, without which matter seems harsh and
stubborn with its blind violent forces of nature. Teilhard
awakens, so to speak, to the power of matter, surrendering
himself in faith "to the wind which was sweeping the universe onwards." As he begins to see matter more clearly, his
mind is illumined, matter reveals itself in its truth, "the universal power which brings together and unites." Every single
element of the world begins to radiate divine love shining
through the everyday stuff of the world. Teilhard claims we
must suffer through the harshness of matter in order to know
its radiance. He writes: "Raise me up then, matter, to those
heights, *through struggle and separation and death*; raise me
up until, at long last, it becomes possible for me in perfect
chastity to embrace the universe" (emphasis added). On the
highest level of union, Teilhard extols matter as the "divine
milieu, charged with creative power . . . infused with life by
the incarnate Word." He exclaims: "Bathe yourself in the
ocean of matter; plunge into it where it is deepest and most
violent; struggle in its currents and drink of its waters. For
it cradled you long ago in your preconscious existence; and
it is that ocean that will raise you up to God."[1] Only at the
highest stage of unitive consciousness does Teilhard come to
a deep intuitive knowledge that in and through matter God
is being born in the world:

> A Being was taking form in the totality of space; a Be-
> ing with the attractive power of a soul, palpable like
> a body, vast as the sky; a Being which mingled with
> things yet remained distinct from them; a Being of a
> higher order than the substance of things with which
> it was adorned, yet taking shape within them. The
> rising Sun was being born in the heart of the world.
> God was shining forth from the summit of that world

[1] Pierre Teilhard de Chardin, *Hymn of the Universe,* trans. Simon
Bartholomew (New York: Harper and Row, 1965), 67, 70, 65.

of matter whose waves were carrying up to him the world of spirit.[2]

How did Teilhard arrive at this mystical embrace of matter? Through long periods of contemplative prayer, nourished by solitude in the desert, slowed time, and attention to the movements of the Spirit, Teilhard came to a deep personal awareness that his life and the world of matter were one, a unity held in being by the dynamic love of God incarnating the world into the Christ. So when Teilhard speaks of a power in matter, he is speaking of the ultimate power that eludes our ability to grasp or measure it. Yet it is a power that is deeply experienced and expressed in the language of awe or wonder, the "dearest freshness deep down things," as poet Gerard Manley Hopkins writes in "God's Grandeur."

Here is the amazing insight that both Francis of Assisi and Teilhard realized: the power at the heart of matter, of a leaf, for example, is the same power at the heart of my life—it is the power of God. I am drawn to the leaf because I am drawn to the truth of my own life—the leaf is a mirror of my deepest self. The center of the leaf and the center of my life are the same center—God-Omega.

For me to contemplate a leaf, therefore, is not simply to withdraw into myself and think about myself; the leaf is not an incentive to find God. Rather, the leaf is God present to me in all its simplicity and beauty. As I contemplate the leaf, I contemplate the source of my life; as I contemplate my life, I discover new things. Teilhard thought that the mystical quest was not a matter of contemplating an established truth but lay in the very act of discovery that illuminates a new truth. I do not leave the world of matter to seek God; on the contrary, the world of matter begins to take hold of me. The God of the leaf recognizes the God in me. Hence, the more I surrender to the power of my own materiality, my embodied existence in which God dwells, the more I am

---

[2] Ibid., 68.

drawn to God in the leaf and the tree and the clouds and the wind. My body and the body of the world are one, and God is shining through this unfolding unity.

The "thisness" of everything that exists is the ineffable center of each particular thing, a center of divine presence inaccessible to "the fantasies of our own mind or the brutalities of our own will" because this "little point of nothingness and of absolute poverty is the pure glory of God," as Thomas Merton writes.[3] From this center God knows me and sees me, even when I do not know or see myself. So too God knows the tree in its treeness and the flower in its flowerness and this being known by God is God contemplating himself in the beauty of each created form, in this tree or this flower. As a tree is known by God, so too does it know God in its own existence simply by being a tree, and in being itself, the tree radiates divine love, which is the ineffable goodness of its own beingness.

In a similar way God contemplates God's life in me, and this gaze of divine love, this being known by God in the deepest center of my self, is the ground of my existence. It is not I who contemplates God; rather, God is contemplating me. Meister Eckhart wrote, "The eye with which I see God is the same eye with which God sees me."[4] God sees himself in me as I come to see myself in God. The perceiver and the perceived are indissolubly one in the universe, in Teilhard's view.

Prayer is the energy of awakening to this radical presence of God. It is the breathing of God's Spirit in me that awakens me to the reality of my own existence. As I awaken to my own reality, I awaken to the reality of the whole of which I am part, the whole that is the universe itself. Although I am drawn to that which I cannot grasp, I am drawn to that which already holds me in the depth of my own beingness. As I am pulled into the power of God, my mind is filled with

---

[3] Thomas Merton, "Le Pointe Vierge," in *Conjectures of a Guilty Bystander* (New York: Image, 1968), 158.

[4] Meister Eckhart, "Sermon IV—True Hearing."

light and my being expands. Such is the power of contemplation.

Theologian Wolfhart Pannenberg describes the Spirit as a field in which one's particular being exists. Each person is like a particle in a relational field of energy. The Spirit unifies the various fields of energy. If this analogy holds true, then the particularity of my existence depends on my energies of relatedness. Prayer expands my field of energies so that the more deeply I am related to God, the more expansive are my relationships, which energize and unite and thus contribute to the work of evolution. Teilhard identified human energy as that increasing portion of cosmic energy, which is influenced by the centers of human activity. While small in comparison to the vastness of the universe, human energy has the capacity to animate and organize into greater levels of complexity. In this way prayer is the energy of evolution because human energy is structurally related to cosmogenesis.

Teilhard's vision of contemplation and evolution is a movement beyond the ego, a surrendering of self to the power of matter. Matter invites me to let go of my self and hand my self over to an attractive power beyond my self. I do not leave the world to find God; rather, God is the power of matter into which I am pulled. From the heart of matter, God calls to the heart of the contemplative; and from the heart of matter, the contemplative is drawn to see more deeply, because matter radiates truth, and in truth, matter finds its meaning. Matter calls to matter; heart calls to heart. To contemplate God-Omega is to enter into matter. As matter takes hold of me and I surrender myself to it, something new breaks open in me, a creative freedom to become something more with matter; and becoming something more in and with matter is becoming my true self, at home in the universe.

Teilhard reframes contemplation within a new paradigm of evolutionary consciousness. As the universe is being formed, the human person is being formed, and as the human person is being formed, so too the universe is being formed. God is the ineffable power of love within every aspect of created existence and the future of that which exists. To give myself over to the power of God is to give myself over to the power of matter, and to give myself over to the power of matter is to give myself over to God. God is truly one with creaturely existence, its creative power, so that as the creature forms and changes, so too does God. Evolution is the rise of God in such a way that God is revealed as evolution progresses. In this respect the fullness of revelation has yet to be known, for God will be fully revealed only at the highest stages of consciousness toward which evolution is oriented.

Teilhard's views on contemplation and evolution are radical and revolutionary. They disrupt our platonic otherworldly religious practices and challenge our stifled individualism and isolationism. We have only to see how monastic life formed and influenced the church to realize that *contemptus mundi* ("contempt for the world") or *fuga mundi* ("flight from the world") are not only dead ends but turn back the cosmic process of evolution toward devolution or fragmentation. Teilhard instead ushers in a truly incarnational perspective on contemplation in a world of energizing matter. Faith and hope in God and the world become faith and hope in God *through* the world.

Martin Laird writes that, for Teilhard, the contemplative is like a sacred door opening on to the universe by which God passes through and spreads God's radiance throughout the entire universe.[5] Contemplation opens my eyes widely to the ineffable depth of matter, a penetrating gaze that gets to the truth of reality. I become "one in heart" with the wind, the moon, the stars, and all the chaotic movements of life, where God is dynamically creating, energizing, and attracting toward more life. Entering into this oneness is a constant movement from my partial, isolated self to a selfless self or

---

[5] Martin Laird, "Contemplation: Human Energy Becoming Divine Energy," *Teilhard Review and Journal of Creative Evolution* 21/2 (1986): 39–40.

that fragment of the whole called "my life," which at the highest level of contemplation is the life of the whole.

Why should we practice contemplation as a form of life? We do so to build the earth, which means to continue the work of creation through faith and hope in this evolving God-world. For Teilhard, faith in God *is* faith in the world. To believe and to have hope is to become one with the world. His incarnational approach to contemplative action means that there is more to building the earth than activism alone. The Christian builds the earth by a certain quality or manner of activity, a way of being in the world, where matter is constantly forming and reorganizing itself on new levels of conscious existence.

Laird uses the term *contemplative energetic* to describe the contemplative evolutionary person in which contemplation is integrated with human activity.[6] Contemplation and action are mutually related, subject to each other, structurally related components of the rise of human energy. The contemplative is one in whom the sap of the world, the energy of matter, flows—the one who embodies a zest for life. The contemplative is a centrating energy of compassion and unity.

Teilhard has constructed a vision in which the human person is vitally related to the formation of the dynamic universe. Contemplation is the process whereby human energy expands and consciousness is maximized. This maximization of consciousness is the expansion of love-energy meshed with the energies of the cosmos. The more contemplation centers the human person in God, the more human consciousness rises and extends the fundamental vital process of evolution through the energies of love. Matter then organizes, physically and psychologically, in more complex ways of greater centration and unity: love attracts, unites, and transforms. Contemplation is the building up of the "contemplative energetic," who centrates, animates, and organizes the universe

---

[6] Ibid., 40.

around a unified center of love, drawing matter into greater levels of unity expressed in the emergence of Christ.

This Teilhardian view of contemplation is complementary to that of Bonaventure and Franciscan spirituality on the whole. For Thomas Aquinas, contemplation is an inner activity of divine union, whereby one expresses the fruits of divine union in the world, a reflective act. But for Bonaventure, contemplation is an ascent into divine love, whereby one hands oneself over in the act of contemplation. Stated otherwise, contemplation is the act of handing oneself over to God. Hence, one is led through suffering and death into matter's dark brilliance of divine light. I think this is what Teilhard perceived as well in his "Hymn to Matter":

> I bless you matter and you I acclaim: not as the pontiffs of science or the moralizing preachers depict you, debased, disfigured—a mass of brute forces and base appetites—but as you reveal yourself to me today, *in your totality and your true nature. . . .*
>
> I acclaim you as the divine *milieu,* charged with creative power, as the ocean stirred by the Spirit, as the clay moulded and infused with life by the incarnate Word. . . .
>
> Raise me up then, matter, to those heights, through struggle and separation and death; raise me up until, at long last, it becomes possible for me in perfect chastity to embrace the universe.[7]

Contemplative prayer grounds us in this letting go process as we engage in a world of change and complexity. For Teilhard, contemplation is to see God in everything, to see that God is calling to us from the world of matter. How we respond in love will matter to the future of God.

---

[7] Teilhard, "Hymn to Matter," in *Hymn of the Universe,* 68–70.

25.

Contemplation and Vision

With the encyclical *Gaudium et spes* Vatican II opened the windows of the church to the complexities of history and the universal call to holiness. A renewed sense of Christian discipleship was kindled. At the same time, a theological renewal took place in which dogmatic theology was reinvigorated by a return to the original sources or wellsprings of foundational writings. *Ressourcement theology* ("return to the sources") brought with it a revival of the Christian mystical tradition and an awakening to the rich texts of mystical writers. Ewert Cousins played a key role in bringing original patristic and medieval mystical writings into the English-speaking world, when in collaboration with Paulist Press, he help establish the Classics of Western Spirituality series and thus opened the doors to the writings of the early and medieval mystical tradition.

One of the advantages of reading the original sources is to see how terms like *contemplation* developed in Christianity. The word *contemplation* is not a Christian term but emerged in Greek philosophy. Plato understood the world of things to be imitations of true reality that lie beyond us in a world of ideal forms. The one who pursues truth must be freed from the senses that shackle the flesh and prevent us from seeing the real. Contemplation is training the mind to focus on divine things. Because the world of matter weighs on us, we must withdraw from the world and turn inward, where the divine light shines. A third-century Neoplatonist, Plotinus, adopted the Platonic scheme and modified it, describing a metaphysical scheme whereby reality flows from the ultimate source of reality, the One, through the realms of the intellect and world Soul, down to the forms of created reality. To search for truth was to pursue a life of contemplation. Plotinus described the path of divinization as a flight of the alone to the Alone, a term adopted by Christian writers.

The first Christian systematic theologian, Origen of Alexandria, was a contemporary of Plotinus and, like Plotinus, saw contemplation as the highest activity of the human person. Contemplation was not a period of silent prayer followed by a burst of activity. Hence, contemplation did not precede action or even give rise to action. In fact, distinguishing contemplation and action in the early church would have been unthinkable. Evagrius, a fourth-century monk, spoke of the active life as preparation for contemplation. The goal of the active life was to purify the passionate part of the soul through discipline and achieve the state of *apatheia* or passionlessness so as to rise in charity.[1] Gregory of Nyssa, one of the Cappadocian fathers, said that contemplation is the heart of Christian discipleship whereby one comes to see the brilliance of God in darkness and know God through the stripping away of all that is known.

For the early writers there was no distinction between being and doing; rather being itself was a form of activity flowing from a deep centeredness in God. Contemplation was the highest activity of Christian life because it was ultimately the transformation of the mind in God. To consider placing a conjunction between "being *and* doing" or "contemplation *and* action" would have been unthinkable. Rather, to live the gospel life was to live a deep prayerful life rooted in the

---

[1] Andrew Louth, *The Origins of the Christian Mystical Tradition* (New York: Oxford University Press, 2007 <1981>), 103–9; John Eudes Bamberger, "Introduction," in *Evagrius Ponticus: The Praktikos*, Cistercian Studies 4, 2nd ed. (Collegeville, MN: Cistercian Publications, 1972), lxxxviii–xc; Bernard McGinn, *The Foundations of Christian Mysticism*, vol. 1, *Origins to the Fifth Century* (New York: Crossroad Publishing, 2002 <1991>), 151–55.

belief that Jesus did not come to change the world but to change the human person. The goal of the life was to acquire a new mind and a new heart and see the world in a new way. The contemplative was to see out of a new center and act out of a new energy of love. After all, if we want a different world, we must become a different people. In the early church the active life was preparation for the contemplative life, not the other way around.

While I do admire the public advocates of social justice who stand as the prophets and martyrs of our time, civil disobedience alone can do no other than act in resistance. Some actions may evoke political change, but many actions simply raise a red flag that something is deeply amiss. Resistant action calls out to the public to become aware of the wrongdoing in our midst. It can raise the consciousness of the need to change, but it in itself is not the change. It is not that we must contemplate in order to act; it is rather that action must lead to contemplation, and contemplation must lead to new vision, and new vision must lead to new structures of relationship.

One of the great mystics of our time, Camaldolese monk Bruno Barnhart, speaks of the sapiential wisdom of our age. He states: "The history of the world in all of its messy, centrifugal energy is not a betrayal of the path of Christ but its lawful and inevitable trajectory."[2] The upheavals and revolutions of modernity, the scientific revolution, secularity, global economics, and the computer age, he writes, are not a betrayal of the spirit but a further creative expression of the dynamic christic ground. If God is deeply entwined with the world, then messy struggle is necessary for creative freedom in love to emerge. The contemplative is one who struggles through to a higher love and lives through the many deaths of the ego to attain freedom in Christ and creatively engage in a new reality.

---

[2] Bruno Barnhart, *The Future of Wisdom: Toward a Rebirth of Sapiential Christianity* (New York: Continuum International Publishing Group, 2008), 205.

Teilhard de Chardin speaks of religious experience as having evolutionary significance through centration of the universe. *Contemplation maximizes consciousness,* he writes, building up a "contemplative energetic"[3] who centrates, animates, and organizes the universe, increasing consciousness. An old woman praying alone in an out-of-the way chapel can move the universe by "entering directly into receptive communication with the very source of all interior drive." In his view, God-Omega exerts its pull upon the universe through the human, who, as the evolutionary spearhead of the universe, has the greatest capacity to be pulled. *Only inner transformation can escape cosmic entropy* and thus centrate energy on higher levels of complexity. Martin Laird writes: "Through divinization the mystic becomes a doorway through which Christ-Omega enters and transforms the world in the Divine Milieu."[4]

I suppose what mystical writers then and now understand is that it is much more difficult to change one's self than it is to change the world. Resisting corrupt political regimes or standing in solidarity with the poor are noteworthy actions, but the most radical action is to stand still before the crucified One, stripped of all ego except the burning desire to love God. Beatrice Bruteau said it best: "An entire attitude, mind-set, way of identifying self and others and perceiving the world has to shift *first,* before any talk of economic, political, and social arrangements can be made. Anything else is premature, useless and possibly dangerous." She realizes, like Teilhard, that "something will explode if we persist in trying to squeeze into our old tumble-down huts the material and spiritual forces that are henceforward on the scale of the world."[5]

---

[3] The term *contemplative energetic* is Martin Laird's. See Martin Laird, "Contemplation: Human Energy Becoming Divine Energy," *Teilhard Review and Journal of Creative Evolution* 21/2 (1986): 39–40.

[4] Martin Laird, "The Diaphanous Universe: Mysticism in the Thought of Pierre Teilhard de Chardin," *Studies in Spirituality* 4 (1994): 222.

[5] Beatrice Bruteau, *The Grand Option* (Notre Dame, IN: University of Notre Dame Press, 2001), 61; Pierre Teilhard de Chardin, *The Phenomenon of Man,* trans. Bernard Wall (New York: Harper and Row, 1959), 253.

To put this another way, contemplation must become the radicality of being itself so that one sees the world with new eyes. We participate in the act of creating when we ourselves open up to being created or re-created by the power of God's love.

I certainly do not mean to refrain from public action, but one who acts must also be able to see a new reality. One eye must look out to the world with its sorrows and tragedies and failures, and one eye must look ahead to what does not yet exist; the two eyes must work together as the third eye of the heart.

Action can lead to a fallacy of misplaced concreteness, as if action alone will actually change structures. The only thing that can change structures is the power of love. And the degree of love that changes the structures of relationships is an unthinkable love. To paraphrase Steve Jobs, it is the crazy ones who think they can change the world, the round pegs in the square holes, who actually do so because they see things differently. If you see what does not yet exist, and you act according to what you see, you will likely be seen as a little crazy, out of center, a misfit or rebel. But if you stay true to what you see because the power of God is the light of your vision, then you will change the world because you yourself will be changed. You will usher in a new reality by your own transformed being-in-love. This, I believe, is the heart of Christian discipleship.

In sum, contemplative vision is the heart of the Christian life by which we are brought into a new reality, connected through the heart to the whole of life, attuned to the deeper intelligence of nature, and called forth irresistibly by the Spirit to creatively express our gifts in the evolution of self and world.

26.

Eucharist and God's Love

These are very strange times. We hover between a virus pandemic, racial injustice, and an economic recession. As of this writing, COVID-19 has pervaded the entire globe. People fear for their lives and their children's lives. Universities have shut down, and stores are closed. Many people are now homebound, and there are fewer cars on the road. The volatility of the stock market has provoked massive selling as people seek to secure whatever monies they have. Hope has lost its vision, and the future is dark.

Despite the events I celebrated a lovely Shabbat meal recently with my Jewish neighbors, Harry and Judy, and their good friends, Michael and Sandy. I was struck by the careful details of the table setting with the lit candles and cloths covering the foods, and then the beautiful prayers of thanksgiving recited in Hebrew over the food we were about to eat. Our gathering was one of community—agape—and during this time of Lent I thought of Jesus dining at the house of Mary and Martha and their brother Lazarus. Although we spoke of the pandemic, our being together and sharing a meal transcended our fears. There was a sense of oneness, unity, as we spoke about many things, including religion. I shared Teilhard's vision on religion and evolution, and they had never heard of such insights before. I told them evolution is moving us toward a new religion of the earth, beyond Jewish, Catholic, Muslim religions, and they blinked twice but pondered this new emergence. Harry and Judy just returned from a trip to Israel and were deeply impressed by the collaborative efforts of Jews, Muslims, and Christians and the new programs being initiated to promote unity. However, Harry and Judy are deeply tied to their Jewish tradition, concerned that younger generations are losing the value of tradition. I agreed to some extent. Each religious tradition has beauty and wisdom within it. We do not want to lose the valuable insights of our ancient traditions and yet we cannot remain in the world of the ancients. Sandy wisely noted that as old traditions fade, new traditions arise. I said that evolution enfolds the best of the old into the new. Nothing is really ever lost; rather, the core values of tradition are taken up and understood in new ways and expressed with new symbols and meanings. We all agreed that tradition is important and that life flourishes in friendship and community.

After I returned home and reflected on our time together, I was reminded of the beauty of personhood. We are born out of love and are created to live in love. How did we fall so far apart from one another, turning friendship into animosity and opposition? Why have we built walls to separate us instead of bridges to unite us? Then I thought to myself:

> You are infinitely near us, O God, within us, among us—the depth and breadth of our very existence. Our panic may be in some strange way a sign of your presence. Apart from you we are random particles of matter struggling for existence. In you, who is the Whole, we know ourselves to be whole. When you are present, we are one. We can pray in a thousand different languages and feel at home together. But when we ignore you, God, reject you, suppress you, or turn you into an idol, we become scattered fragments of matter without meaningful life together. Only when we move toward one another do you emerge as the center of our lives.

Community meals remind me that nature is a relational whole. Twentieth-century science opened new windows to the realization that nature is porous, permeable, and chaotic. Complex cellular life organizes according to principles of systems rather than individual function. Neural nets, algorithms, and genetic codes are just some of the ways that nature has developed tools to calculate the processes of life in ways that are open to more life. Nature does not work according to fixed essences or autonomous existents. Rather, nature is a choreographed drama or, better yet, a symphony of unfolding life, where even the seasons express the different movements of nature's flow.

As I write, we are approaching spring here in North America, and once again tiny buds are piercing through what appeared dead during the course of winter; the dried bark of the maple tree has been a disguise for the flourishing life within. Every aspect of nature has a part in this symphony—even the Coronavirus. Everything works rightly when it functions in its natural habit. Everything gives God thanks and praise. As Sara Thomsen sings in the opening lines of "Canticle of the Feathered Ones":

Canticle of the Feathered Ones

Hymn of the hermit thrush
A song in the holy hush
A lake in the sake of the sun.

Vireos in the vestibule
Warblers wait in the wings
A finch begins to sing
The water, a sparkling jewel

Kyrie eleison, kyrie eleison.[1]

But when the niches of nature are disrupted, exterminated by bulldozers for the purpose of building shopping malls,

---

[1] From the recording "Song Like a Seed," © 2014 Sara Thomsen. Harmony Works © 2019 Sara Thomsen. Inspired by the poem "Sunday Morning" by Anne Stewart of Ely, Minnesota.

or forests are stripped of their communal life for housing developments, the natural habitats of nature are confused and disoriented. Have we ever considered the silent war we have declared on nature in the last few hundred years in the name of progress and development? Are we aware that we created conditions of mass migration of species? Even viruses and bacteria can become lost in space as their simple lives are disrupted. They can be forced into exile, impelled to take up residence in "foreign lands" where they are not at home. Have we considered that our blind ambition for money and power has provoked climate change, melted glaciers, displaced species, and disrupted the natural flow of life? We have become overconfident in our ability to conquer but lost the sense of who we are within the wider world of nature? Lack of self-knowledge, according to Bonaventure, makes for faulty knowledge in all other matters. Maybe it is time to take a good hard look at ourselves and ask if we have had a part in the emergence of deadly viruses. Have we considered our part in the disruption of natural habitats? Finding a new home can be difficult, especially as a foreigner in exile. Even the life of a virus can be disrupted by global warming; forced into exile by climate change, mutation is quite possible, as it tries to adjust to a new environment. I am not trying to vindicate COVID-19, but I am saying that we may not be totally innocent in this matter.

Many people ask why God does not save us or spare us from tragedy and death? Others interpret these times as the beginning of the apocalypse, thinking that God is standing ready in judgment, as we approach the end times. Still others say that religion is the problem and not the solution. All of these ideas are foreign to God, who is Life itself. God has nowhere to go but to remain with us because God is our Creator; the work of God's hands is the fabric of our lives. God does not punish us because we are selfish at times; rather, we punish ourselves by losing faith in God, who remains faithful in love because the world is integral to God's life, and God needs the world to be truly who God is. Always present, faithful, and empowering in love, God is absolute oneness in love and will not rest until we are joined together fully in love—not just every person but the whole world, the planet, the galaxies, the entire universe—when God is all in all, bound in a single embrace of love.

Teilhard lived through many harrowing experiences. His expeditions took him to difficult areas where he endured blistering heat, icy blizzards, poor food, sandstorms, snakes, flash floods, marauding bandits, civil war, political intrigue, bribery, and drastic policy changes leveled by unstable governments. No matter how trying the times, he continued to develop his vision of hope in God. He realized God will not save us; rather, we must save ourselves by waking up from our deep sleep and engaging in evolution, in the movement of love toward greater wholeness. To be saved is to be made whole by the power of love.

God is always present at the doors of our lives, but we must answer the knock on the door: "Listen! I am standing at the door and knocking; if you hear my voice and open the door, I will come to you and eat with you, and you with me" (Rev 3:20). We do not hear God knocking because we are too busy trying to protect ourselves in our isolated existences. We hoard all the goods we can buy and shut our doors. We fear a knock on the door because we do not want to encounter a stranger. Without trust in God, we worry about being eaten alive, like the children in William Golding's *Lord of the Flies*.

Yet Christianity is precisely focused on eating the Body of Christ, which leads to my further thoughts on the Eucharist. Someone recently wrote to the Omega Center and asked how to make sense of the Eucharist in light of Teilhard's vision of evolution. What does *consubstantiation* and *transubstantiation* mean in an unfinished universe? In light of dinner with Harry and Judy, and Michael and Sandy, I can say Eucharist is the sacrament of friendship. At that dinner the depth and presence of God's love in my life met the depth and presence of God's love in their lives—different people from different traditions meeting together in the breaking of bread and the sharing of wine, united in the transcendent power of love. And from this center of convergent goodness God appeared in a new way, a new light, a new understanding, a new power of friendship and unity: "For where two or three are gathered in my name [Love], I am there among them" (Mt 18:20). This is Eucharist in an unfolding universe: the bringing together of diverse elements, people, ideas, values, and traditions in the breaking of bread and the sharing of wine, toasting together to the fullness of life. When we share life together, God appears in our midst as Life itself, and we rise up together beyond the resistant forces around us and within us. This is the Body of Christ.

Christianity can help us realize that death and resurrection are part of the evolutionary path toward wholeness, letting go of isolated existence for the sake of deeper union. Something dies, but something new is born—which is why the chaos of our times is, in a strange way, a sign of hope. Something new is being born within. Breakdown can be breakthrough if we recognize a new pattern of life struggling to emerge.

The old structures of power and greed are fighting tooth and nail against the forces of evolution, but they are dying out. We are living in the midst of a great epochal shift, and we need a new religious awareness to help us realize that God is the power of this great shift; absolute Love can never remain incomplete or partial. Realizing that God is change itself (for perfect Love is always in movement), we must overcome our selfish selves by reaching out to others in love, reaching across the tables, so to speak, that divide and separate us. Awakening to God's presence can help us know that we need one another; we belong together. Life takes on a new fullness when it is celebrated together. To know we are not alone is the beginning of our peace; and when we live in peace, we live in freedom. If we realize we are not alone, then death has no power over us. Even if we succumb to physical death, we will live in a new power of cosmotheandric life, the life of the whole in which we will find our truest personhood for all eternity. Jesus said, "I am the resurrection and the life. Those who believe in me, even though they die, will live" (John 11:25). I believe in the resurrection and the life.

God is struggling to breathe new life into this world—to gather all peoples, all creatures, all that exists, into a new unity so that we may become a new earth community where God is at home in the unfolding of life and the dynamism of love. I suppose it will take a number of existential threats for us to realize that God needs us to be God, and we need God to be us.

We are in this together, and no matter what happens, God is Love itself. And God will always be our future.

27.

Teilhard's Troubled Worship

*J*t is almost five years since Pope Francis's encyclical "*Lau-dato Si*' (*On Care for Our Common Home*), and unfortu-nately nothing has changed with regard to global warming. The statistics continue to show rising temperatures, and this trend is predicted to have dramatic consequences on future earth life. Even the prophetic voice of Greta Thunberg has done little to change the state of affairs. Climate-change activists continue to protest against the present policies (or lack of), but these actions too are ignored. The pope's plea and Greta's cry for a sustainable future fall on deaf ears. Statistics do not move us to change, and prophets go unheard.

The church continues to issue documents on global warm-ing, as well as immigration, economics, and other current issues, but few people are reading these documents. It is sad to think that if the church died tomorrow, the world would likely express its sympathy but not attend the funeral.

In past ages Christianity was a creative force for change; in the twelfth century the Vatican was the closest thing to Silicon Valley, initiating social reforms and economic policies that shaped Western Europe. Today the church has apparently lost its power to persuade. It continues to issue insightful writings, but they are dead letters falling on blind eyes and deaf ears. The glory days are past, and Christians are breathing the fumes of history. In fact, much of Chris-tianity lives on the laurels of history and nostalgia. We talk and preach as if we are still the noble center of the universe and special creatures of God, not the most recent arrival of a universe that is 13.8 billion years old.

The writings issued by the Vatican are a strange blend of patristic sources and medieval Thomism with a dollop of modern science and culture. The past gives a warm fuzzy feeling of the power of God, divine providence, moral order, and the beauty of wisdom. We long for what was because we can no longer make sense of what is. Indeed, the church clutches the great thinkers of the past, mostly the Greek philosophers and medieval theologians, as if they just appeared in the evening news.

God never changes, according to Teresa of Avila. How could God change with fixed and eternal truths? God has little choice but to remain unchanging. The well-worn words of Julian of Norwich inspire us to stay the course of this medieval fortress: "All shall be well." But all is not well. The church is no longer an active, vital force in the world. A church deaf to the cries of the world, Raimon Panikkar writes, is unable to utter any divine word. What is the world crying out for? A green earth? Water justice? Immigration rights? Or is it crying out for new bodies, new brains, and new minds, all promised by the prophets of Silicon Valley?

In a provocative essay entitled "Salvation by Algorithm," Yuval Harari outlines the new religion of technology.[1] Harari is an Israeli historian and professor of history at the Hebrew University of Jerusalem and also author of *Homo Deus: A Brief History of Tomorrow* and *Sapiens: A Brief History of Humankind*. His ideas have been widely discussed. His secularist and agnostic view shows a cursory understanding of religion and spirituality, and yet his insights are poignant.

Harari writes: "The most interesting place in the world from a religious perspective is not Syria or the Bible Belt, but Silicon Valley." He says that is "where hi-tech gurus are brewing for us amazing new religions that have little to do with God, and everything to do with technology. They

---

[1] Yuval Harari, "Salvation by Algorithm: God, Technology, and the New 21st-Century Religions," *New Statesman* (September 8, 2016).

promise all the old prizes—happiness, peace, justice and eternal life in paradise—but here on Earth with the help of technology, rather than after death and with the help of supernatural beings."[2]

The established religions may boast of a divine mandate, he indicates, giving them a fixed essence of eternal and unchanging truth, but they "have no fixed essence. They have survived for centuries and millennia not by clinging to some eternal values, but by repeatedly pouring heady new wine into very old skins."[3]

"Heady new wine" is a very interesting term, for it highlights a lot of Catholic doctrine and preaching; Greek terms explained in long homiletic drones. While Catholics may claim allegiance in the millions, strength is not in numbers, according to Harari, but in bold, new creative ideas. In his view the train of *Homo sapiens* is leaving the station, driven by the engineers of Silicon Valley: "Whereas during the Industrial Revolution of the 19th century human beings learned to produce vehicles, weapons, textiles and food, in the new industrial revolution of the 21st century human beings are learning to produce themselves. The main products of the coming decades will be bodies, brains and minds."[4]

Brett Robinson also draws a relationship between religion and technology in his book *Appletopia*.[5] The transcendent design of the Apple Store, according to Robinson, fits a historical pattern wherein the dominant technology of an age acquires a sacred status. In the Middle Ages the great cathedrals were packed with people searching for an experience of transcendence; today, the Apple Store is packed with people looking for the same experience. Cars, like computers, were built to transport the user, he writes—one moves the body

---

[2] Ibid.

[3] Ibid.

[4] Ibid.

[5] Brett T. Robinson, *Appletopia: Media, Technology, and the Religious Imagination of Steve Jobs* (Waco, TX: Baylor University Press, 2013).

and the other moves the mind. Both machines changed our relationship to space and time.

Apple devices encourage self-expression by inviting spontaneous creativity and personalization, according to Robinson. Religious communication uses metaphorical language because it proposes realities that cannot be grasped directly. The invisible workings of the metaphysical realm are understood in relation to something sensible and concrete. Religion is communicated through stories, symbols, art, and analogies. The rhetoric of technology resembles religion in its need for metaphors to make the unknown sensible. Artistic engineers create easy-to-understand metaphors: folders, desktops, icons, and memory to name just a few. Part of Steve Jobs's genius was finding the metaphors that resonated with the uninitiated user. In the age of screen worship, media technology has become a determinant of contemplative habits.

The advertisements for Apple are emblems of a culture that has adopted technology as a de facto religion, a religion that celebrates the cult of the individual. Media devices are the means by which we communalize our concerns and ritualize the practice of self-divinization by procuring the powers of omniscience and omnipresence granted by a global communication network. Whether or not we agree with the interpretation of technology as a new place of religion, it is worth noting why technology lures us at all. Transcendence, self-creation, and connectivity are just some of the underlying dynamics of technology. With the touch of a button the physical and the metaphysical realms merge before our eyes. A godlike status is granted to those who gaze on the infinite streams of information running across their screens.

Computer technology takes its cues from nature. When twentieth-century physics exploded with a new understanding of matter and energy, the concept of the field was born. Cybernetics and information soon came to explain the complexity of dynamical systems working in tandem with the environment. In order for science to accept Einstein's theory of relativity and the discoveries that followed, old paradigms had to be discarded or placed aside.

Science, in a sense, ditched Aristotle, Aristarchus, and Copernicus, and opted for Darwin and Einstein. Newton's laws of space and time could not hold up to Einstein's equations. Matter and energy, Einstein realized, were two forms of the same stuff. Paradigms change, Thomas Kuhn writes, when the data no longer fits the equations; Newton's world was seen in an entirely new way by Einstein, and the world itself took on a whole new meaning. Science changes because we change our perspective; we see nature in new ways. What we see is that nature is elusive, replete with mystery. Nature is not fixed and static but dynamic and unfolding, which is the essence of evolution.

28.

Can Consumer People Be
Christmas People?

Christmastime on the planet of the rich is a time of consumption. In fact, what we realize around this time of
the year is that we have a lot of stuff—so much stuff that
many people donate to charity (as tax write-offs) or simply
opt out of giving gifts. The planet of the rich is a planet of
material things. We can now buy everything whenever we
want at the touch of a button or the swipe of a card, so gifts
become a nuisance for some people. A frequent response
to the question, "What would you like for Christmas?" is,
"Don't get me anything; I already have too much stuff," or;
"Please don't buy me anything, I don't *need* anything." (Who
said Christmas was about need?)

What seems most apparent in our consumer culture is the
spirit of self-sufficiency: thank you for your offer, but *I* have
too much stuff; *I* will buy it when *I* need it; *I* give my stuff
away when *I* want to. Christmas on the planet of the rich
is consumerism run wild, resulting in either mass hysteria
of unmet needs and desires or absolute control of the flow
of goods. Is it possible to really celebrate Christmas in a
consumer culture?

Christmastime means gathering around the birth of Jesus,
the unfathomable mystery of God's self-gift. As Christians
we believe that God gives Godself to us wholly, completely,
absolutely, and without reserve in the birth of an infant: a
tiny, poor, humble, Jewish baby born in the squalor of a

stable with a birth announcement given to shepherds by angels saying: "Here lies the Most High. *This* is God, and God is like *this*, not greater or more glorious or more powerful than this tiny, poor, helpless infant." The gift of divinity is hidden in humanity, and there is no return policy.

Philosopher Jean-Luc Marion, in *God without Being*, plumbed the mystery of God as the gift of being itself. Marion recognizes that God does not give gifts. Rather, God *is* gift, and the gift of God is hidden in the concrete reality of existence, the everydayness of form and beauty: the human face, the tiny babe, kittens and rabbits, trees and fawns, tiny ants and stars. Everything that exists bears an excess of gift, flowing from the heart of divine Love, revealed in the depth and beauty of each thing and all things.

Saint Francis of Assisi had a deep sense of the gift of God in creation. Everything spoke to him of God—flowers, trees, rabbits, earthworms. Even his difficult brothers revealed the gift of God's love. Francis did not go around saying, "Oh, thanks, but I have enough flowers" or, "Please do not send any more fruit, because everyone keeps sending me fruit and I have too much." Rather, his first words were, "Thank you."

Francis was not so much interested in material things but in the *gift* symbolized by the material good. A gift is something freely given, a personal expression of love flowing from one person to another, symbolizing a bond of unity or belonging together. Francis received graciously from others because each gift was, in a sense, given by God, whether the gift was a mountain, a palace, a small donkey, a loaf of bread, or a smile. For him, the gift expressed the giver. The gift itself was not so important as was the giver of the gift because each gift freely given is a gift of God.

A gift graciously received creates a shared life, a *sacrum commercium* or sacred exchange between divinity and humanity, and thus a bond of unity. Every gift given and graciously received is an act of creating a new future together. Because he encountered the manifold gifts of God in the everyday experiences of life, Francis lived with a deep sense of gratitude. He began each new day with the simple words, "Thank you." Life in God is about living in the gift of life; and to receive graciously is to live in the flow of life abundant.

Of course, the greatest gift for Francis was the gift of Jesus Christ. One of the most profound episodes in his life is the Christmas scene at Greccio in the year 1223, three years before his death. Francis wanted to set before his bodily eyes the inconveniences of the infant, "how he lay in a manger, how, with an ox and an ass standing by, he lay upon the hay where he had been placed." After describing the preparations, Francis's biographer, Thomas of Celano, writes: "The manger was prepared, the hay had been brought, the ox and ass were led in. There simplicity was honored, poverty was exalted, humility was commended, and Greccio was made, as it were, a new Bethlehem."[1] However, the Christmas scene contained no statues or players representing Joseph, Mary, or the child. It was not merely a drama, but a reenactment of the divine drama. Francis was convinced of the reality of the descent of the Word, divinity bending low to assume our fragile humanity. He arranged to have a mass celebrated over the manger and preached on the Christmas gospel. He sought to connect the nativity scene with the present incarnation of the Lord as word and sacrament. Christmas *is* Eucharist, and Christians are to be Christmas people.

The key to Christmas for Saint Francis is poverty. The incarnation is the movement of God to poverty, to indigence and dependence on others, thus revealing the divine good throughout creation—even in people we do not like. Scholars have known for a long time that Francis of Assisi rarely spoke of poverty in terms of material things. His poverty was not about want or need; it was about dispossession. The poor person is not one who lives without things but without *possessing* things. The one who possesses cannot receive,

---

[1] Thomas of Celano, "The Life of Saint Frances," in *Francis of Assisi: Early Documents,* vol. 1, *The Saint,* ed. Regis J. Armstrong, J. A. Wayne Hellmann, and William J. Short (New York: New City Press, 1999), 255.

because one is constantly clinging in a way that grasps and controls. Francis made every effort to live materially poor so that he could live spiritually poor. Material poverty was not an end in itself but a means to living in radical dependence on God and thus on one another, since God lives in our neighbors, our family members, community members, and the people we meet on the street or in the mall.

What Francis sought to do was to live—not without things, but without grasping and clinging to things. When every aspect of life is gift, including our material goods, we live with a sense of gratitude. Whether we purchase the item ourselves or receive it from another, it is a gift freely given in the moment to use, to share, to reflect the goodness of human work. To live *sine proprio* ("without possessing") is to have an inner space of freedom where we can receive from the other without trying to control or manipulate the other, for this is how God comes to us, in the hiddenness of the other.

Etty Hillesum came to a similar insight in July 12, 1941, as she awaited her inevitable deportation from Nazi-occupied Amsterdam. She writes: "But one thing is becoming increasingly clear to me: You cannot help us, that we must help You to help ourselves . . . that we safeguard that little piece of You, God, in ourselves. . . . You cannot help us, but we must help You and defend Your dwelling place inside us to the last."[2] Etty Hillesum, like Francis of Assisi, lived in the gift of life. They were Christmas people.

Can a consumer world really celebrate Christmas? Is it possible to receive the manifold gifts of God when we reject or seek to control the gift of the other? The simple answer is no. Consumer Christmas turns the personal gifts of divine love into commodified goods. On one hand, Christmas is a wonderful time for family gatherings, renewed friendships, and tokens of gratitude, all of which reflect the deep relational nature of being itself. We love to be loved, to be

---

[2] Etty Hillesum, and J. G. Gaarlandt. *An Interrupted Life: The Diaries, 1941-1943; And, Letters From Westerbork* (New York: Henry Holt, 1996), 178.

needed, recognized, singled out, but it is an illusion to think we are in control or that we can control gifts by either receiving them or rejecting them.

As long as we condone a culture of possession, we reject the gift of life. We may celebrate consumer Christmas, but we are not Christmas people. The person who possesses and controls cannot receive, and the person who cannot receive cannot give thanks. Christmastime should be an awakening of consciousness that *all* is a gift freely given and that our task is to receive in poverty of spirit and give thanks. The lowliness of Christ's birth shows us where the gift of divinity is to be found: in the poor, the humble, the forgotten, the weak, the simple, the laborer, the immigrant, the unwed, the old, the dumb ox, and the smelly sheep. The Most High God, whose incomprehensible love cannot be purchased or downloaded, bends low to embrace us in our frail humanity so that we might be raised up into the heart of divinity. Francis knew by the end of his life that *all* is a gift. Even his sufferings and physical ailments were gifts given by a God of generous love. Only by way of suffering can love be refined, as iron is molded in fire.

The frivolity of consumer Christmas on the planet of the rich is an illusion that cannot last. We may "shop until we drop" or refuse to exchange gifts because we have no need for more stuff, but we are missing out on the significance of Christmas itself: the gift of life freely given and graciously received. Everything is a gift—every drop of water and grain of sand, every card sent or candy exchanged. Christmas is not doing for others; rather, it is being done unto. This is the heart of Mary's *fiat*: "Be it *done unto me* according to your word."

We do not call the shots; we receive the grace of divine love that empowers us to do new things, to give birth to new life. It takes an expansive inner space of poverty for the seeds of new life to be planted. When we own nothing, we are ready to receive everything.

A spirit of consumption can only lead to death. By consuming one another and the things of the earth—the natural resources of oil, water, air, wind, and soil—we continue to take in to the point of being bloated, unhealthy, and diseased. We are living in the illusion of self-sufficiency, where even the best of us can feel self-righteous. But what has been freely given can be freely taken away. Our God is a jealous God, whose overflowing generosity cannot be outsmarted or stripped by Google or Amazon. One has only to think of the story of Job to realize this reality.

We are facing a precarious future because we are enslaved by consumption. The only possible outcome for a consumption-obsessed earth, where the footprint of the United States is 23 percent larger than the earth can regenerate, is a great suffering. It will come, and we will not know the day or the hour. But this great suffering will be a great gift, because we will once again receive graciously from one another without demands or constraints. Then we will live in the true spirit of Christmas.

29.

Internet Easter

The COVID-19 pandemic has significantly changed human life around the globe. No matter what country, culture, language, gender, or religious tradition, everyone is affected by this crisis. Social distancing and face masks are now routine preventive measures. The internet and virtual communications are saving us from total isolation and keeping education and businesses on track, albeit at a much different pace than normal.

We developed computer technology in the 1950s, following the Second World War and the failure of modernity to achieve utopia. Thanks to discoveries in science, technology, and communications, we began to understand how nature works through dynamical systems, information, and cybernetics. The creation of thinking machines was a way of extending human thinking beyond human biological life. The launching of the first website, on August 6, 1991, enhanced the lure of the computer. Cyberspace became sacred space, as we enfolded technology into our cultural landscape. What is less apparent is that the advent of the computer age and public awareness of ecological destruction due to human interference took place around the same time. The term *cyborg* (cybernetic organism) was coined in 1960, and in 1962 Rachel Carson wrote *Silent Spring*, alerting the public to the environmental toxicity of pesticides.

Computer technology evolved at an exponential rate, while the ecological movement has had fits and starts, gaining some momentum in the ensuing decades but never capturing the attention in the same way that computer technology did. We bought into Apple computers, Microsoft, and Google and made them very wealthy companies; we forgot the needs of the earth, as we googled our way through the internet. Some scholars claim that computer technology exploded because religion became stagnant and out of touch with the world. Doctrines of original sin, heaven and hell, final judgment, and salvation from a depraved world instilled genetic fear that still lingers. God was remote from everyday life, and religious authority was the mouthpiece of God.

The internet alleviated these religious trappings by opening up an infinite space of information where one could find a slice of heaven on earth, explore personal identity and develop friends around the planet through cyberspace. Religion shrank while technology expanded. Consumerism fed off the new technology like a parasite, eager for us to buy our way into heaven. The parallel lines of religion and technology left the earth bereft of tender care. We developed "geomnesia," a lack of remembering our deep roots in the earth. Religious otherworldliness became technological cyber-spaciousness, as we eagerly sought to transcend the finite boundaries of earthly existence.

Thomas Berry reminded us several decades ago that we belong to the earth, that the earth does not belong to us. We have now disrupted so many ecosystems and niches due to unbridled power and the pursuit of wealth that there is likely a silent war that has erupted between nature and humans; we have become the most unnatural species on the planet. If viruses and bacteria could speak, they would probably say, "We lost our way and cannot find our natural homes anymore, for they have been leveled and replaced by buildings." I think the systems of nature have been communicating among themselves for quite some time, perhaps forming a federation of earthlife to consider the extent of human destruction and probably planning a global human coup d'état in the twenty-first century. I would not be surprised to learn of such a discovery; for nature is made for the flourishing of life and will do whatever it takes to achieve its purpose.

We find ourselves in a new reality now with facemasks and self-imposed exile. Is this a temporary disruption to our lives, or a sign of what to expect in the twenty-first century? My own inkling is the latter. It would be naive of us to think that a new vaccine will solve our pandemic problem; we will need a storehouse of vaccines in the twenty-first century to cope with possible future pandemics. There are displaced pathogens all over the globe, and with the complexity of information abounding, genetic mutations and zoonotic spillovers will continue to take place. Science and technology can achieve wondrous results, but disrupted nature will oust our scientific knowledge.

Pierre Teilhard de Chardin anticipated a significant global crisis in the mid-twentieth century, but no one paid attention to him because his writings were considered unorthodox. However, he saw that evolution is an unyielding process toward greater complexity and consciousness. Nature plows through dead ends and cataclysmic events toward new unities because nature works as a whole; life can only flourish as a whole. Teilhard saw the rise of computer technology as part of nature's evolving wholeness. By the mid-twentieth century we had blown up the world (literally) through the violence of war, but nature worked through the destruction to find new ways to connect toward new wholeness. One way was the rise of the computer. Teilhard learned of the computer in 1950 and was astonished by its capacity to link human minds. He describes a new layer of thinking mind, the noosphere, emerging through computer technology. He speaks of the noosphere as the realm of the *deeply personal* through *convergence,* or the bringing together of diverse elements, organisms, and even the currents of human thought: "The Future universal cannot be anything else but the *hyperpersonal.*"[1] By *hyperpersonal* he means that our ability to unite with others and expand human consciousness will be enhanced by computer technology. More consciousness

---

[1] Pierre Teilhard de Chardin, *The Phenomenon of Man*, trans. Bernard Wall (New York: Harper and Row, 1959), 260.

is the basis of more unitive life, as minds gather in shared thoughts and ideas. Teilhard saw the insufficiency of science to bring about a new level of collective consciousness. "It is not tête-à-tête or a corps-à-corps we need; it is a heart to heart."[2] Hence he saw that the rise of the computer could also bring a renewed sense of religion, one that embraces the earth as the place to find God.

I thought of Teilhard as I participated in the Palm Sunday liturgy on the internet. It is not the same as going to church and sitting in a pew, but I found myself less distracted and more focused on the readings and prayers. A number of Catholics have voiced concern that they cannot receive the sacraments, especially the Eucharist, via internet mass. We have strayed very far from the early Christian church and the Eucharist as agape, the significance of a meal as the expression of shared love, a meal of thanksgiving for the goods of the earth, family, and friends. Eucharist is not about "eating Jesus"; Eucharist takes place wherever two or more are gathered in an ineffable depth of love. God dwells quietly within. The practice of daily communion is relatively modern. For the first thousand years of Christianity reception of the Eucharist was at most several times a year. In the Middle Ages people had great reservation about receiving the Eucharist (for various reasons), and the church had to mandate at the Fourth Lateran Council (1215) that Christians receive the Eucharist at least once a year. Francis of Assisi (as well as Clare) likely followed this practice—and they were holy people.

Christian liturgy has become a routinized, mechanized pious devotion, an idolatrized form of worship that has depleted the real value of the sacraments. We do not partake of the sacraments "to be saved" by consumption; we partake of them to be freed. "God has come to his people and set them free," according to the words of the *Benedictus*. The sacrament of the Eucharist is not a meal to be consumed but

---

[2] Pierre Teilhard de Chardin, *The Future of Man*, trans. Norman Denny (New York: Image Books, 1964), 75.

a meal to be shared and offered to others. "See what you love, become what you see," in the well-known words of Augustine. Eucharist is more of a quantum entanglement of our lives and God's life, a sacred exchange, so that our lives becomes God's life and God's life becomes our lives; this is the only way God can break into the world. Not to be conscious of this entanglement is not to realize the meaning of the words "the body of Christ" and the response, "Amen," so be it—I concede.

Our narrow, provincial religious thinking has suffocated God, squeezing out God's life from the everyday cracks of the world. Teilhard was acutely aware of this narrow thinking. God is within, he said, at the tip of my pen, in the tiredness I feel, in the silly joke someone told, in my darkest fears, and in my basking in the sun. Our task is to awaken to this deep presence of God, to find our freedom in this God of love, and to help create the world unto the fullness of love. To do so we must have a vital relationship with the living God.

To this end I think internet religion may be a sign of a new religious consciousness on the horizon. It is not the same as the old religion; it can lack the warmth of the smells and bells and friendly neighbors squeezing their way into the pew. And yet, online I can attend different liturgies around the world; I can explore different religious traditions; I can hear prayers and participate in rituals I would never otherwise discover. Internet religion may be God's way of saying: I am much larger than you think. I actually enjoy different languages and rituals. I can be found in a thousand ways, and I cannot be boxed into a concrete structure, whether a church, a temple, a formula, or a decree. All of these are human constructions that in the past were helpful but in our age have hindered and at times alienated us from our capacity to unite. Now we are in the midst of a pandemic, and the internet is pushing us toward a new planetary community, sharing our fears and hopes online, joining in a common concern for our future.

Jesus was about community. The word *church* or *ecclesia* means to be called out of our partial lives and called into a new gathering of people. Francis of Assisi felt called to rebuild the church. He began with rocks but then realized the call was much deeper, and he began to rebuild the church by transforming his life in Christ. Jesus said, "Destroy this temple, and I will raise it again in three days" (Jn 2:19). He was not speaking of a structure but of his own body. Toward the end of his life Francis sang the "Canticle of the Creatures," a doxology in which all earthly life gives praise to God, a liturgical celebration of the cosmic Christ, divine love shining through the sun, moon, stars, water, earth, and all creatures. For Francis, the whole universe became the place to find God, and he traveled by foot across the mountains and valleys, stopping periodically because he saw the dazzling presence of God in a rabbit, a bird, a bunch of flowers. When he found twigs on the ground in the form of a cross, he would fall down and prostrate himself in prayer.

We do not go to church to find God; we find God by going into the world. Church is a symbolic gathering of what God is doing in this earthly life. The earth is holy, people are holy, plants are holy, trees are holy, animals are holy, and all life is called into a greater wholeness, a unity in love that is compassionate, forgiving, peaceful, and unitive. The earth is the one glorious moving mass of interconnected energy fields in space. Religion is the awareness that this incredible planet has infinite purpose and meaning, a future fullness of life, a wellspring of life that exceeds our human capacity to imagine.

As we enter into the Triduum online, we remember Christ's suffering and death by becoming "membered to" the sufferings of earth life—to be "membered to" Christ in what he endured in the past and now in the present; to be "one with" the suffering God in the suffering of humanity, especially those deeply affected by the COVID-19 virus. We are "membered to" those who have died from the virus, the healthcare workers working around the clock to save lives, and all those who are keeping our present structures viable.

We are "membered to" all those who have lost their jobs, who are struggling at home, who are falling back into addictions, who are resorting to violence out of desperation. God is dwelling in all these areas of life. It is where Easter is taking place.

God did not spare his Son the agony of the cross; divine love does not hold back for itself. God is not a consumer but a giver of life. God suffers in the suffering of the weak, the fragile, and vulnerable. God suffers not out of need but out of an abundance of love. And it is because God suffers with us, an absolute fidelity in love, that nothing can destroy life. Because of God's absolute fidelity in love, a love unto darkness and death, a love that cannot be vanquished, God is our hope and our future. How to find God as the ubiquitous love-energy of planetary life must be our concern in the twenty-first century. Without this energy, all other energy sources will be depleted.

A new God-consciousness calls for a rebirth of religion. Internet religion may be the first sign of a new religious consciousness and convergence in our age. Being online and not in a church will give new meaning to the words: "He is not here; he has risen" (Mt 28:6). And where is this risen Christ? Everywhere and all around us—in you, your neighbor, the dogwood tree outside, the budding grape vine, the ants popping up through the cracks. The whole world is filled with God, who is shining through even the darkest places of our lives. To "go to church" is to awaken to this divine presence in our midst and respond in love with a yes: Your life, O God, is my life and the life of the planet.

During these days leading up to Easter we have an invitation to go to church in a new way, by praying before the new leaves budding through dormant trees or the wobbly flowers by the side of the road pushing through the solid earth. "Praised be you, my Lord, through Brother Sun . . . Sister Moon . . . and Mother Earth," Francis sang in the "Canticle of the Creatures." We too can sing with the air we breathe, the sun that shines upon us, the rain that pours down to water the earth. And we can cry with those who are mourning, with the forgotten, with those who are suffering from disease or illness, with the weak, with the imprisoned. We can mourn in the solidarity of compassion but we must live in the hope of new life. For we are Easter people, and we are called to celebrate the whole earth as the body of Christ. Every act done in love gives glory to God: a pause of thanksgiving, a laugh, a gaze at the sun, or just raising a toast to your friends at your virtual gathering. The good news? "He is not here!" Christ is everywhere, and love will make us whole.

Vespers

Forgiveness arises
Out of creative love;
A conscious intention
To be part of
The act of new creation,
Ex nihilo
Living on the edge of
The next moment of life.

Suffering—yes
But the suffering of returning
The good that the unforgiving heart
Wants to steal and covet
And punish.
If we relate only to the
Past deeds of others, we live
With dead remains;
We breathe
But we are not really alive,
Not really living.

For to live is to love,
And to love is to create.
Forgiveness is the act of
Making a new future.

"Let the dead bury their own dead,"
Jesus said.
How can the dead bury the dead?
That is how far down the unforgiving heart goes,
into the absurd dark hole of deadness,
where nothing breathes.

Jesus's last breath was a word of forgiveness,
He broke through the barrier
of the hardened heart and loved
to the end that never ends.

Forgiveness *is* resurrected life,
The power of hope joins the power of love
And gives birth to the power
Of the future.

30.

Radical Forgiveness—
Lessons from Nature

ature is fickle. Just when you think you know some-thing about something else, say another human person, a tree, or your new cat, you are taken off guard because the other can spring from the plane of the predictable and do surprising things. Just about a month ago we adopted two six-month-old kittens who had struggled through the first few months of life. We brought them home from the shelter, thinking that these two would be fragile and weak, but in a month's time, with lots of food and rest, they have come alive. Despite their fragile beginnings, they are playful and carefree and remind me of nature's creative resiliency. They romp down the hallway, throwing their toys into the air, as if the abandoned alley never existed.

We expect nature to be fixed and predictable, yet we are constantly challenged by nature's subtle playfulness. Buddhists speak of nature's impermanence. Things change from moment to moment, never fixed in the endless flow of life. Hindus speak of *lila,* divine creative playfulness throughout the cosmos. Despite our will to control nature or perhaps preserve the things of nature from destruction, nature cannot be controlled or preserved. It is the "nature" of nature to change, to birth new life, life unto life, which is why nature is our mother.

The most appropriate word to describe nature is *relationship.* Life is relational all the way back to the Big Bang. A modern commentary on the Big Bang might begin: In the beginning is relationship and out of energized relationships new life emerged. The physical universe is a luminous web of interconnectedness. Space is not an empty container for atoms to bounce around like volley balls in the air; rather, space is filled with overlapping fields of energy. Nature thrives on energy.

Modern science is filled with examples of deep relationality, from the double-slit experiment to the Krebs cycle, nature is an unending stream of dancing systems. Things are constantly appearing and disappearing, as if everything, from quarks to compounds, is undulating in the folds of space-time. Nature is not a lump of clay or a set of inert building blocks. Rather, nature is an unpredictable, at times erratic, highly charged, light-filled electronic three-ring circus of spontaneously creative matter darting from one energy level to another, unyielding forces of attraction continuously drawing elements together. Pierre Teilhard de Chardin called this persistent force of attraction *love-energy*, and he said that love is the true stuff of the universe.

If nature is relational, then nature is constantly sharing secrets. Relationships are not static but channels of flowing energy in which information is darting back and forth across the boundaries of things. Energy flow is particle talk, as if particles might say to one another, "Let's stay for a while," or "It's time to converge." There is a mindfulness in nature that vitalizes the direction of nature's flow. In the Newtonian cosmos, matter had no purpose or intention; it held no room for spirit or consciousness. Newton's physical world was set against the mental, and in turn, the mental came to be seen in terms not physical. Quantum physics changed this story considerably. Today we realize that consciousness is integral to all aspects of cosmic life. No consciousness, no matter. This has led scientists to speculate that the universe is brimming with consciousness, from the most elementary particles to vast galaxies, from amoebas to Bach and Einstein.

The openness of nature to creativity means that no aspect of nature can be constrained by form or boundaries.

Given a sufficient amount of time and the right conditions, created entities will transcend their limits, especially if the limits constrain rather than liberate the element or subject. Transcendence means to go beyond the boundaries of self-existence. In a sense, transcendence complements creativity, because the movement beyond self means enhancing the capacity for new relationships and thus for new things to happen. The combination of creativity and transcendence enables the things of nature to evolve, to move to new levels of complexity and thus new degrees of relatedness.

Nonhuman nature has a built-in capacity to let go so as to flow into new life; perhaps we might say that it has an intrinsic forgiveness factor. Relationships can be damaged because things happen, but there is a real propensity for bonding and group coherence among many different types of biological species. I watch my two kittens, for example, fight over food or attention, yet shortly after being embroiled in conflict, they reunite and sleep together in the same little bed with its soft furry lining.

Christianity is based on nature, actually a union of natures. The Chalcedonian formula describes the person of Jesus Christ as two natures, truly God and truly human, one in nature with the Godhead and one in nature with humankind, a mysterious unity of natures that could be described as a hybridization of natures. God's deeply relational creative love is poured out through the divine Word into space-time, rendering this creative, birthing process of nature an entangled image of divine love-energy. The creativity and openness of nature reflect the creativity and openness of God.

It is easy to see why Jesus was not so rigid about nature; his life exemplified the openness of nature to new life. Indeed, the Gospels reorient human nature toward Godly fulfillment by unleashing human religiosity from the constraints of duty, law, tradition, and group mentality. God loves nature, and anything that opposes nature opposes God.

Lent is a good time to reflect on what it means to be part of nature. When do we become rigid and entrenched in our ideas? How do we try to control our relationships? The season of Lent calls us to check our human nature and our capacity for life-giving relationships. When we are unconscious of this capacity, we are prone to cut ourselves off from others, especially if we have been hurt. Lenten conversion is centered on forgiveness. Jesus tells Peter that he is to forgive not merely seven times (a perfect number) but seventy-seven times (Mt 18:21–22), that is, an endless number of times.

Forgiveness is a Big Bang attitude; instead of allowing past hurts to absorb us in a black hole of unhappiness and inner turmoil, nature teaches us to let go. Often we want to hurt those who have hurt us by stripping the good within them. To forgive is to return the good that belongs to the other. We cannot undo past hurts or injustices, but we can create new bonds of relationships, embarking on a new level of life open to new life in God. Forgiveness is creative; it has the potential to birth new life. It liberates and revitalizes us for life, opening us up to the wonders of the present moment, releasing within us the creativity and playfulness of our human nature. Forgiveness restores love within us in a way that we can begin to see the world with new eyes. One who forgives realizes that the past cannot be undone and that the only real moment of life is now. Radical forgiveness is radical loving, making a choice for life, to be part of this dynamic evolution toward more being and consciousness, to help create a world of unity, justice, and peace. The practice of forgiveness is our most important contribution to the healing of the world.

We humans can easily fall prey to being "victimized," resentful, angry, self-righteous, and therefore seldom at peace with one another because we cannot forgive one another. Forgiveness begins in the heart. We cannot forgive others if we cannot forgive ourselves and let go of our divisive thoughts. To heal our inner woundedness is to know God's power of love is stronger than death, a love overflowing with future life.

Jesus does not ask us to preserve nature but to return to nature: "Look at the birds of the air; they do not sow or reap or store away in barns, and yet your heavenly Father feeds them. Are you not much more valuable than they?"

(Mt 6:26). We are to learn the patterns of life that give birth to new life. Nature can teach us how to rise from the dead because the whole of nature reveals the astonishing power of the risen Christ. So let us put past hurts behind us and return any good that we have stolen from another. Let us return to the playful creativity of nature and celebrate the gift of life. Resurrection is happening now, in our midst, taking concrete form every day. To experience resurrection is to be fully conscious that love heals and life only knows life. Practice resurrection.

31.

Costly Love

In the 1960s, Gordon Moore, the cofounder of Intel, predicted that computing power would double every two years, increasing evolution at an exponential rate. Technology has radically changed our lives to the extent that we are evolving rapidly but not evenly. We can no longer presume the human person is a homogenous entity; rather, every person is in a flow of becoming but the rate of flow differs depending on each person's ability to expand in consciousness. Evolution is developmental time, and it depends on a variety of factors including environment, history, culture, and engagement in the local milieu.

The interwoven use of technology in our daily lives, however, has disrupted our biological adaptation to evolution. For example, studies today show that the human brain is changing due to continuous internet use. Brain capacities such as memory and thinking are being outsourced to Google. Because the brain is a "use it or lose it" organ, the obsessive dependence on technology is causing the human brain to lose memory capacity and also the capacity to think deeply. Moreover, our sense perceptions are being changed insofar as the lines between virtual and real are being erased. As a result, our emotions of love, compassion, fear, and aggression are being altered. The Pavlovian response to email dings or texts is inducing hyper-anxiety, impulsive behavior, and narcissism. We have some serious questions to face, not so much "what are we doing with our technology?" but "what are we *becoming* with our technology?" Everything we are is being rearranged by technology.

The influx of technology into our daily lives also has profound implications for religion. Scholars recognize that the rise of modernity and the split between science and religion has led to a disenchantment with nature. As science began to master the spaces of the natural world, God was pushed out. Modern science has systematically dismantled Western understandings of sacred space, leaving God, heaven, and the souls of the dead with no particular place to go. The understanding of and mastery over physical space, from astrophysics to genetics, has meant a loss of spiritual space in the physical world.

But the fact is, we long for transcendence; we are *capax infiniti*; our constant urge is to reach for the stars. But if science has conquered space, where shall we turn? For what shall we reach? This is where technology has stepped in to fill the gap left by our disenchantment with nature. The cyberworld provides an arena of transcendence; it fills a psychological and religious void in modern life. And this is why the ecological crisis will continue to deepen as technology expands, because the light of divinity in nature, as Saint Francis perceived, is now found online in the unlimited arena of virtual reality.

While a discussion on technology and ecology is essential, my purpose for raising the import of technology for our age is that we are losing consciousness of what it means to be human. We are spending the majority of our waking hours in front of a screen or tethered to a device, and we are losing contact with nature, not only with the world of trees and flowers but with the nature of being human. We are less tolerant of one another, more emotionally reactive, and increasingly unable to cope with the complexities of our age. Our addiction to technology is causing us to unmake the world at an alarming rate. Perhaps most important, we are losing the capacity to love by way of forgiveness and reconciliation; that is, we are losing the ability to transcend our partial lives by way of love in order to create a new future together. Political, economic, and social unrest continues to spiral, thanks to technology, and we cannot find a means to slow down or turn in a new direction.

We have within the Christian tradition the wisdom of the cross, the inscrutable mystery of God's unconditional love in the midst of suffering and death. The cross seems, on one hand, foreign to us, and yet it is our deepest reality. There is no new life without suffering and death. Bonaventure saw the cross as the most explicit expression of God's love. Christ crucified discloses the heart of God in the heart of the universe. The cross expresses the mystery of God's absolute love hidden in the finite frailty of the human person. The humility of the cross reflects the humility of God. In light of the crucified Christ, Bonaventure indicates that being is embodied love—an agapic love that possesses nothing for itself but rather gives itself entirely and completely to the other. *To be* is to love, and *to love* is to be in relationship. Teilhard de Chardin would agree; love is our deepest reality. The universe is grounded in love.

But if love is our truest nature, and technology is changing that nature, how can we renew our deepest reality of love? This is a question for our age and an important one to engage. For the type of love that mends broken hearts is not superficial; it cannot be controlled electronically by the touch of a button. It is a decision to love beyond what is beneficial or satisfying to one's ego; it is to love by way of sacrifice. This type of love requires a greater love at the center of one's being—love of God, love of neighbor, and love of self, the triadic structure of love that is at the mysterious core of our personhood. It may be that we have to hit rock bottom before we discover this love deep within us, the realization that we belong to one another because we belong to God, and without one another we cannot find our wholeness of life in God.

The movie *The Railway Man* powerfully portrays the type of costly love that is needed in our age. It is the true story of Eric Lomax, a British soldier captured by the Japanese in the fall of Singapore in 1942 and subjected to slave labor in the construction of the notorious "death railway" from Thailand to Burma. Lomax miraculously survived to confront his torturer forty years later. During his time as a prisoner, Lomax was savagely beaten and tortured by the Japanese soldier, Nagase; and even after he was freed, had returned home, and had married, he was driven by an unabated obsession for revenge against Nagase. He eventually returned to Japan to meet his former torturer in order to seek justice and confront the man who destroyed his life. But when he finally came face to face with the aging Nagase, the old man had changed with time. Encountering one another in the same place where death had prevailed, Lomax met a man broken down by years of remorse. Nagase admitted that the Japanese had been brainwashed to confuse violence with success. The final scene is a light-filled resurrection of life, as if seeing Jesus being raised from the dead by the power of love. Each man begins to walk toward the other, meeting in the center of the road. Without hesitation, Nagase bows low before Lomax, expressing deep sorrow for his actions. Lomax is torn between hate and forgiveness; he realizes that he must let hatred go if there is to be any hope of new life. It is hard to imagine that one could befriend a former torturer, but indeed that is how the story ends. The two men who were mortal enemies found their humanity in one another through the power of love and the will to forgive. Through their lives the power of love and the power of forgiveness were visibly intertwined.

This type of love, costly love, cannot be found in virtual reality or managed online. It requires all that we have and all that we are. It requires our utmost attention, our hearts, and our wills; this type of love requires total self-gift. Love is not looking at the other, but it is looking together in the same direction, releasing the other from the grip of hate and allowing the good of the other to shine through, insofar as that good is oriented toward a new future. Where there is love and forgiveness, there is hope for a new reality.

God will not mend our broken hearts without us, but God will continue to be with us, constantly challenging us with the question, What do you want? We are being invited into deeper levels of love and forgiveness in our own time, because this is our deepest reality. Love is the energy of creativity and imagination because love stretches us beyond ourselves to reach for the stars. How we choose to love in a world of distrust will affect our future, a future that we will create together or not at all.

32.

Time to Become Ultrahuman?

According to planetary life, we have been celebrating a new year for a very long time! The fact that we are here after such a long time is remarkable and hopeful. It tells us about nature and the power of life to prevail despite massive violence, suffering, and tragedy. Nature is not fixed or static; rather, nature has the capacity to do new things. What drives nature into a new future?

Pierre Teilhard de Chardin said that evolution is the rise of consciousness. Consciousness may be the creator and governor of matter; the background of the universe may be mindlike. Teilhard thought deeply about consciousness and cosmogenesis. He linked these together through the most advanced form of consciousness known in the universe, namely, the human person. He intuited a deep relationship between the power of spiritual energy and the energy of cosmogenesis.

Teilhard saw that human energy is structurally related to the overall cosmic energy and assumes three distinct forms: incorporated energy, controlled energy, and spiritualized energy. In his view, spiritualized energy is the most highly developed expression of human energy. Human energy in its spiritualized form has an organizing quality of cosmic significance. Human energy affects the structural development of the cosmos; it is the spearhead of cosmogenesis.

Teilhard's understanding of evolution was influenced by the French philosopher Henri Bergson and his idea of an *élan vital* ("vital impulse") at the heart of evolution. According to Bergson, nature is conservative. Human societies change very little, he said; the changes they undergo remain at the surface and do not deeply affect their nature. Bergson suggested that nature resists change and tends toward closed groups. He claimed that the aspiration to be an open society, an inclusive [human] community, is quite literally against nature. The change for an open society or a new level of human community rests on the human capacity for turning against nature, something that can be done only if we know what this nature is.

Paola Marrotti writes: "Bergson calls for a strategy that aims at countering nature from within, looking for ways to go against natural tendencies, to change and modify their direction with the help of other tendencies or tools. That is, to counter nature with its own weapons, so to speak."[1] We can go against nature because its stability is conservative but never absolute. Nature's stability is a tendency relative to and dependent on the more essential tendency to change.

Bergson leaned toward a supernatural presence in nature to account for nature's becoming, an idea that influenced Teilhard. Rather than an elusive presence, however, Teilhard identified this supernatural principle in nature as *Omega*. The principle of Omega is the presence of something in nature that is wholly other than nature; it is distinct yet intrinsic, autonomous, and independent; it is deeply influential on nature's propensity toward complexity and consciousness.

This Omega principle accounts for the *more* in things, for example, the *more* in society than the individual. Omega is the most intensely personal center that makes beings personal and centered because it is the attractive center of love that empowers every center to love. As the principle of centration that is within, Omega escapes entropy so that it is ahead of nature as its prime mover. Omega therefore emerges from the organic totality of evolution and is the goal toward which evolution tends.

---

[1] Paola Marrotti, "The Natural Cyborg: The Stakes of Bergson's Philosophy of Evolution," *Scottish Journal of Philosophy* 48, Spindel Supplement (2010): 16.

Teilhard identified the Omega principle with God and spoke of God at the heart of evolution as its source and goal. God-Omega is the center at the heart of every center, the vital hidden presence at the core of every living entity. Thomas Merton also spoke of an inner divine presence which is the source of our unity and wholeness:

> At the center of our being is a point of pure truth, a point or spark which belongs entirely to God, which is never at our disposal, from which God disposes of our lies, which is inaccessible to the fantasies of our own mind or the brutalities of our own will. This little point of nothingness and of absolute poverty is the pure glory of God in us. It is so to speak His name written in us, as our poverty, as our indigence, as our dependence, as our sonship. It is like a pure diamond, blazing with the invisible light of heaven. It is in everybody, and if we could see it, we would see these billions of points of light coming together in the face and blaze of a sun that would make all the darkness and cruelty of life vanish completely.[2]

Both Merton and Teilhard realized that there is a center of absolute Love, a Oneness and wholeness within us, that is the source of our personal wholeness and the cosmogenic evolution toward unity in love. Each in his own way indicated that contemplation is essential to the active life. The contemplative is one who holds the universe together through the energy of love.

Teilhard placed an emphasis on contemplation as the main source of vitality for cosmic evolution. He believed that contemplative prayer is cosmic power because in some way the contemplative mediates God's creative power. In *The Divine Milieu* he tells the story of someone who enters a chapel and sees a woman at prayer:

---

[2] Thomas Merton, *Conjectures of a Guilty Bystander* (New York: Image, 1968), 158.

All at once he sees the whole world bound up and moving and organizing itself around that out-of-the way spot, in tune with the intensity and inflection of the desires of that puny praying figure. The convent chapel had become the axis about which the earth revolved.[3]

For Teilhard, this inner power, the power of God-Omega, is awakened through contemplation; it orients all time and space into a unified field of love by which the whole cosmos becomes more unified in love.

The ancient philosopher Plotinus wrote in his *Enneads* that contemplation has cosmic significance because, through contemplation, all things are held together. Teilhard and Plotinus believed that contemplation is linked to the organizing processes of the universe. If we want to evolve into a new world, a new cosmos, then we must discover the inner universe.

Humanity has the capacity to evolve to the next level of evolution, which Teilhard called the ultrahuman; however, it needs "the help of a new form of psychic energy in which the personalizing depth of love is combined with the totalization of what is most essential and most universal in the heart of the stuff of the cosmos and the cosmic stream—and for this energy we have as yet, no name!"[4] Martin Laird suggested that the term "contemplative energetic" could aptly describe the overlapping zones of human activity and contemplative activity, vital zones of energy related to the process of cosmogenesis.[5]

Instead of placing all our faith in science and technology to lead us into a better future, perhaps it is time to attend

---

[3] Pierre Teilhard de Chardin, *The Divine Milieu: An Essay on the Interior Life*, trans. William Collins (New York: Harper and Row, 1960), 133.

[4] Pierre Teilhard de Chardin, *The Activation of Energy* (New York: Harcourt Brace Javanovich, 1963), 227.

[5] Martin Laird, "Contemplation: Human Energy Becoming Cosmic Energy," *Teilhard Review and Journal of Creative Evolution* 21/2 (1986): 39–40.

to the mystics, who tell us that meditation or contemplative prayer may be the most important sources of energy for human evolution. We continue to be faced by the same problems that are dissipating our energies: global warming, pandemics, the threat of nuclear war, the migration crisis, racial opposition, political factions, and economic instability. We are worn out trying to solve these problems by analytical means, and we are exhausted by the repetition of these problems, which not only perpetuate themselves but deepen. Our human energies are thinned out, and we are at the brink of a human energy crisis. We are exhausting our capacity to centrate our lives in a radiating power of love. The energy that is ours to co-create the world is being squandered on globalized superficiality and fake news; petty ideals are fueling globalized indifference.

We have the capacity for a new world, and the energy for this world is already within us. It is the presence of God-Omega. Science has discovered some of the secrets of nature, but we do not yet know the secret of our own lives. We have mapped the genome and measured the planets, but we are ignorant about our own interior universe. We need to discover the vast inner layers of the human person, the realms of mind and consciousness—and contemplative prayer is a good place to start. Perhaps in this New Year we can turn inward by sitting still, meditating, listening to the silence, comfortable in the dark as we seek the light, stretching toward the One who is the power of all life to bear new life. It is time we set out our goals on becoming ultrahuman.

Compline

It is hard to say what death is like
While still in breathing skin.
Daylight fades or suddenly
Disappears
And the unknown mystery
Of life
Springs up from the abyss of the soul and
Becomes Final, Fullness, Eternal.

The whole universe carried within
Is now brought to completion in
The Act of Death.
The Last breadth is now the First Act
of real freedom.
The source of life is now
The goal of life;
All relationships are gathered up
in a moment of profound reverie.

The Me forming through
Life's loves and struggles
Is now revealed and permanently
Sealed on the heart of You—
For better or worse
Richer or poorer,
My "life" is now permanently entangled
With Your Life,

217

And the life of the Whole.

In death, my heart ceases but
My life continues in a glorious way
The way of Divine Love;
The process of my becoming spirals on.

I now join in the Great Work of Love
Living beyond the bounds of space-time
Permanently sealed on the heart of God
Whose only work is "loving the world";
And in this work
I shall endure
Forever.

33.

Evolve or Be Annihilated

In 1953, Pierre Teilhard de Chardin wrote an essay entitled "The Agony of Our Age: A World That Is Asphyxiating," in which he pointed out that after eons of slow expansion, the human species has entered a phase of compression. Every part of the globe is inhabited by the human species, and we are all now confronted by a new reality on this earth.

What we see is a wellspring of humanity competing for limited resources and land. This flood of sheer humanity, Teilhard writes, is seeping through every fissure and drowning the rest of us. We are becoming enervated both intellectually and physically, from lack of solitude and of nature. And the internet and mass media have made the world even smaller by providing instant news every moment of the day.

We find ourselves in a disagreeable closeness of interaction; a continual friction between individuals who are alien or hostile to one another; a mechanization of persons in the corporate collective mentality of big business; and an increasing insecurity of daily life, with constant threats of terrorism and violence invading our waking hours. There are too many of us in too little room.

The truth is, it is just like a train in the rush hour—the earth is coming to be a place on which we simply cannot breathe. And this asphyxiation explains the violent methods employed by nations and individuals in their attempt to break loose and to preserve, by isolation, their customs, their language and their country. A use-

less attempt, moreover, since passengers continue to pile
into the railway carriage. Instead of being exasperated
by these nuisances from which we all suffer, or waiting
vaguely for things to settle down, would we not do
better to ask ourselves whether, as a matter of solid
experiential fact, there may not possibly be, first, a reas-
suring explanation of what is going on, and secondly,
an acceptable issue to it?[1]

Teilhard goes on to say that we are witnessing an explosion
in the biosphere that has been released suddenly from the
rest of the living mass and is now piling up to the point of
being crushed on the closed surface of the earth. In order
to escape the asphyxiation that threatens us, the remedies
proposed are either drastic restriction on reproduction or
mass migration to another planet. Since the latter is unlikely
at this point, and the former does not ensure a sustainable
future, we must look for the relief without which our zoo-
logical phylum cannot survive, not in a eugenic reduction or
in extraterrestrial expansion of the human mass but in an
escape into time through what lies ahead. The one thing we
hold together is the future and we must allow this reality to
engage us together.

   We have not accepted evolution as our story. We treat evolution as a conversational theory or something that belongs
to science, as if science is something separate from us and
outside our range of experience. Politically, we have fiefdoms
and kingdoms; socially, we have tribes and cults; religiously,
we have hierarchy and patriarchy. There is nothing that sus-
tains, supports, or nurtures human evolution.

   By evolution, I mean simply that change is integral to life.
We are becoming something that is not yet known. To live in
evolution is to let go of structures that prevent convergence
and deepening of consciousness and assume new structures

---

[1] Pierre Teilhard de Chardin, "Reflections on the Compression of
Mankind," in *The Activation of Energy* (New York: Harcourt Brace
Javanovich, 1963), 342.

that are consonant with creativity, inspiration, and development.

Evolution requires trust in the process of life itself. There is a power at the heart of life that is divine and lovable. In a sense we are challenged to lean into life's changing patterns and attend to the new patterns that are emerging in our midst. To live in openness to the future is to live with a sense of creativity and participation, to use our gifts for the sake of the whole by sharing them with others.

There is something about this word *evolution* that frightens people, as if evolution renders us less human or less special as human. We do not talk in terms of evolution; nor do we think in terms of evolution. Our everyday lives are conceived as static and fixed, as if it has always been this way and should always remain this way. But this type of thinking is completely erroneous.

The truth is, evolution is not a series of radical leaps from one species to another but a gradual emergence of traits, along with genetic mutations and adaptations that result in new genetic identities and traits. The process of evolution reveals nature to be in a constant flux of openness to new forms, new relationships, and new processes that not only sustain but optimize life in the face of environmental changes, especially climate change.

Evolution reveals that nature is much more interactive, creative, and adaptive than the human species alone can attest. There is a constant urge in nature to transcend toward higher levels of complexity (degrees of relationship) and consciousness. Teilhard states that evolution is the fundamental process of all aspects of life, leading him to assert that every system, if it is to survive, must conform itself to evolution.

I am amazed at how many people resist evolution, even though just about every aspect of modern life runs on principles of evolution, from the newest smartphone to the latest diet. Technology is probably the best indicator of evolution. We have our smartphones, iPads, and computers, and with these devices we can access different worlds at the click of a button. Gordon Moore, cofounder of Intel Corporation, predicted in the 1960s that the computer chip would grow exponentially, that is, every two years we would evolve to a new level of computing power, which is exactly what has happened.

This growth in computing power has changed us significantly; we create the tools, and the tools create us. Those born before 1985 might remember the phone on the wall with a cord. One could only walk so far with the phone in hand. I remember when the first cellphone went public. It was about a foot long and weighed a few pounds, but it was completely novel. Then came the laptop computer, another unbelievable innovation of human ingenuity, and then the anticipation of holding a palm-sized computer in hand. When I heard about the cellphone-computer back in the early 1980s, I thought it seemed incredible, if not impossible. Would we really be able to talk to someone and then send them a message, too, all with the same device?

Now, some people might say, these devices just make phone calls easier or communication faster. But technology is an extension of biological evolution; human nature has an infinite capacity to imagine new things. If I dream of something, and focus my mind on the object of my dream, and create this object and make it real, then I can merge with the object of my dream and what was once a dream is now a reality. This is the human dimension of evolution. What we imagine, we find a way to create, and what we create is what we become.

Our world is now smaller than ever because we are wired together—and while this affords new growth, it has also bred more competition and consumerism. Our attention spans are limited and diverted by extending our waking selves into our devices. The amount of information we are confronted with each day has exploded into an exhausting level of information because we do not know how to make sense of all the information flooding our overworked brains. Essentially, we do not know how to think as people in evolution.

The challenge of evolution is essentially stifled by two main systems: religion and education. Religiously, we have faith systems confined to old cosmologies and entrenched doctrines. In education, we are still operating on the scientific principles of the German university, where objective knowledge and specialization are not to be confused or mingled with subjective experience or spirituality.

We are educated to think as closed-system specialists, and we are religiously sheltered by medieval dogma. From these two main systems arise all other systems in the world. If we are thinking out of old boxes and praying to old gods, it is no wonder that evolution frightens us and we resist its forces.

But this challenge of evolution differs among age groups. Digital natives tend to be entrepreneurial and more creative. The postmillennial *digital native,* a term coined by Marc Prensky in 2001, is emerging as the globe's dominant demographic. Digital natives, or those born after 1985, are wired differently from analogues, or those who grew up with wall phones and black-and-white television. Digital natives think like their networks and social media sites; they think in terms of connections and communication rather than across lines of ontological distinctions.

There is a greater sense among the postmillennial generation that things can change, that the world can become a better place, and that we must use our gifts to help create this new world. This is evolutionary thinking. Resistance to evolution comes primarily from the older analogue generations, who fear being connected, that is, being closer together as different tribes of people, different religions, different cultures, different languages, and different worldviews.

Yet evolution is pressing in the direction of convergence and globalization, and the political forces of the world resist this change at a high price. Anti-evolutionists want to remain stable, fixed, tribal, and nationalistic. They want to avoid convergence, which includes shared space, shared resources, shared policies and shared power. Teilhard warned that we must converge by way of evolution, or we will annihilate ourselves.

This is our threshold moment, and we need to get on board with evolution. If we get nothing else straight about our present moment, it should be this: stability is an illusion. The ancient wisdom of Heraclitus reminds us of life's endless activity: The only thing that is permanent is impermanence. No one steps in the same river twice. If there is no permanence in the present, then the only real stability is the future. The Buddha intuitively grasped the notion of evolution by advocating detachment, not necessarily the act of giving up the things of this world, but rather accepting and being consciously aware that nothing is permanent. So too, Francis of Assisi taught his disciples the principle of dispossession, not living without things but without *possessing* things (*sine proprio*). Evolution requires revolution, and one of the main forces that must make a complete turnaround is religion.

At a UN-sponsored conference in 1975 a group of religious leaders drew on Teilhard's ideas of planetization in their statement calling on world religions to come together to harness the spiritual energies of the earth:

> The crises of our time are challenging the world religions to release a new spiritual force transcending religious, cultural, and national boundaries into a new consciousness of the oneness of the human community and so putting into effect a spiritual dynamic toward the solutions of world problem.[2]

We are all complicit in the present forces of devolution by which we are thinning out our resources and draining our energies to converge. Our refusal to see, our inability to hear the new sounds of a new world arriving, and our refusal to rearrange our comfortable lives are taking their toll. We suffer the sin of fixity and stability. And the price to pay for this sin will be steep. At some point the rope tautly drawn between big money and political power will snap. We will

---

[2] UNESCO Symposium, New York City, October 24, 1975, cited in Ewert H. Cousins, "Teilhard's Concept of Religion and the Religious Phenomenon of Our Time," *Teilhard Studies* 49 (Fall 2004): 20.

not be able to hide in our glass houses because we will all be gasping for the little air left to breathe.

Thomas Berry summed up the problem of our age in a single sentence: "We will go into the future as a single sacred community, or we will all perish in the desert."[3] We are starting to feel the effects of perishing in the desert. It is time to come together to work for what we share together, the future, into which we are being fearfully but irresistibly drawn. This is the true test of our faith, what we really believe in, because God *is* the power of the future.

---

[3] Thomas Berry and Thomas Clarke, *Befriending the Earth* (New London, CT: Twenty-Third Publications, 1991), 43.

34.

Hope in a Time of Crisis

The world is in a heightened state of volatility. Fear of the Coronavirus has created global unrest. Environmental warming continues to show its effects. In *Until the End of Time* physicist Brian Greene declares that there is no purpose to the universe; it is just "my particle army carrying out quantum mechanical marching orders."[1] What, no purpose? We are just particles in the universe having bad karma? There is no meaning to anything? How utterly unhopeful.

But we do hope. It is the main impulse of life. Why do we awake to a new day anticipating that things will improve? What accounts for the hope that lies within us? If life were simply about random particles interacting with no purpose or meaning, death too would be meaningless. Yet, Teilhard de Chardin noticed that there is something else going on in the universe. He thought deeply about these questions and came to some of his greatest insights in the trenches of World War I. Serving as a stretcher bearer, surrounded by wounded and dying soldiers, Teilhard realized that the destruction of war signaled something breaking through in the world, something not yet realized but coming to birth. This was not naive optimism but a realization that war is destructive but not final. The violence of war is horrible, but out of the rubble life finds ways to rise up again.

---

[1] Brian Greene, *Until the End of Time* (New York: Penguin Random House, 2020), 153.

We treat death as an evil, yet death is integral to life. "Things perish with a passing over in which the sacrificed individual also flows in the river of life. . . . Each is a blood sacrifice perishing that others may live," philosopher Holmes Rolston writes.[2] On the level of nature, death functions as part of the dynamic flow of open systems. Life breaks down, flows into the wider stream of activity, and is taken up in new ways. New order emerges from the existing order. Systems break down because something new is being formed.

Death and life mark the dynamic process of evolution. Life moves from simple to complex organisms where relationships increase and consciousness rises. There is really nothing in nature to warrant this dynamic flow save the open nature of systems themselves. Teilhard identified the power of change as Omega, the ultimate energy of wholeness, centration, and fecundity. God is Omega, the ultimate depth of all that exists; yet God is more than anything that exists. God is the future fullness of life to which we and all life are drawn. Everything is in movement and oriented toward ultimate life because God is love, and love is ultimate wholeness-in-movement and the future toward which we are moving.

It is because this power of divine love is at the heart of life that evolution requires more than mere matter to explain its direction toward wholeness and self-reflective consciousness. The creation story in Genesis does not begin with humans but with the most fundamental feature of the universe— light. And not just physical light but metaphysical light, psychological light, emotional light, spiritual light. Light is a synonym for consciousness, and consciousness is the inner dimension of matter itself. Panpsychism, which proclaims the fundamental reality of consciousness, opens a new window on Anselm's ontological argument: God is that than which no greater can be thought, the ultimate horizon of consciousness itself. God is the ultimate depth of consciousness which is present at the heart of matter from the "beginning." In this

---

[2] Holmes Rolston, "Kenosis and Nature," in *The Work of Love,* ed. John Polkinghorne (Grand Rapids, MI: Eerdmans, 2001), 59.

respect God and matter belong together; it is incarnation all the way back to the beginning. Religion is the depth dimension of matter. Since institutional religion consolidates this depth dimension into paradigms of transcendence, religion is at the heart of evolution. Religion and evolution belong together, Teilhard writes: "The religious phenomenon, taken as a whole, is simply the reaction of the universe as such, of collective consciousness and human action in process of development."[3] Religion has a cosmic and biological function long before it has a human function; without a viable religious depth dimension, evolution cannot proceed toward its capacity for greater wholeness.

If we doubt that religion and evolution belong together, we can trace the emergence of religion in human evolution through the rise of axial consciousness. Whereas pre-axial religion is cosmic, mythic, ritualistic, and communal, axial religion is individual, solitary, and transcendent. World religions, including Christianity, are first axial religions. All of them developed a set of doctrines, rituals, and beliefs based on the human person as individual in pursuit of transcendence. Western Christianity compounded axial religion by consolidating it into a religion of the empire, thus injecting fundamental Christian principles into all areas of human life, including politics, economics, and science.

Twentieth-century science revolutionized our world and, in doing so, left institutional religion on the platform of the train station. We have changed because our fundamental understanding of reality has changed, and yet we are more adrift today than a hundred years ago. This is where the religious dimension of evolution plays a significant role. Without a viable religious dimension to cosmic evolution, science has nowhere to go, no real aim. Science has been operating on principles of evolution for over a century, while religion has simply ignored evolution, as if it is just a theory.

---

[3] Pierre Teilhard de Chardin, "How I Believe," in *Christianity and Evolution,* trans. René Hague (New York: William Collins and Sons, 1971), 118–19.

The Catholic Church in particular has maintained a critical distance with regard to modern science, open and interested but protective of its core doctrines, which remain static. A God who is not related to evolution, however, cannot be a God of evolution. We simply cannot cut and paste medieval theology onto twenty-first century cosmology or adapt the theology of Thomas Aquinas to fit the contours of an open-systems universe.

One of the biggest obstacles to planetary wholeness is religion. Without a renewal of religion for a world in evolution, evolution has no compass, no cosmic GPS system, leaving the human community subject to the blind forces of nature. And this leads to the most volatile situation of all, a world created for wholeness yet spiraling downward because there is nothing to guide it, no organic purpose or meaning.

We can ignore the fundamental drive of evolution and what modern science has been telling us for the last hundred years. We can make believe we still live in a three-tiered universe and aim for the reward of heaven. We can feel good about ourselves by going to church, practicing centering prayer, giving to the poor, building homes for the homeless, and feeding the hungry. We have made religion into a self-serving, self-saving enterprise: do good, avoid evil, and practice the golden rule. But in doing so we reduce religion to a self-service counter in the same way that Brian Greene has reduced the universe to interconnected particles, leaving the whole of earth life without depth, breadth or future.

We have entered a new axial age of consciousness, one that is communal, ecological, cosmic, informational, interbeing. It is no longer about the human person in need of salvation; now it is about being part of a dynamic whole where deep interconnectedness marks our lives. Since the actions of one affect the many, so too the salvation of one is the salvation of the many. We are either saved together or not at all. Technology has advanced this new age of consciousness at a rapid speed; the train of human evolution has left the station, and institutional religion is not on it. Teilhard realized almost a hundred years ago that any religion that focuses only on individuals and heaven is insufficient. People are looking for a religion that gives meaning to human achievements, a religion that will kindle cosmic and human evolution and a deep sense of commitment to the earth. He speaks of the need for a new religion that could activate and energize us for a forward movement of love. Traditional religion is too tied to old cosmologies, he says, to have any real effect for the planet. God has been too small to nurture in us a zest for new planetary life.

So we are confronted with a very big decision that we may not realize on a daily basis. Do we want to maintain our old religious doctrines, practices, rituals, and beliefs while we are catapulted into a second-axial posthuman existence? Do we really think religion will slow this process of change or perhaps temper it with a set of moral values? This can easily make religion into a form of escapism. But there is no escape from where we are going. We are created for wholeness, and our planetary life will not rest until it rests in wholeness, the dynamic interconnectedness of all life. To resist the forces of evolution is to create a downward spiral of unraveling, which is what we are encountering today. Our present systems were built on the needs of the individual, and now they are battling against the forces of change. Nature is pushing us to evolve into interplanetary life, but human structures resist this convergence and struggle to remain independent.

Teilhard was deeply aware of this reality and devoted himself to bridging faith and evolution. In his view Christianity can be one of the most vital resources for earth because its basic faith claim is that God has entered into materiality. The God of evolution is in evolution. Teilhard thought that God and world form a complementary whole, that God affects the world and the world affects God, and that one cannot exist without the other. What would the world look like if we practiced Christianity as an unfinished religion in an unfinished universe? What if God's becoming depends on deep relationality, co-constructive meaning, integral systems dynamically engaged with the environment? What might worship look like? What form would prayer or meditation take? What would a church that actually preached and proclaimed a God at the heart of integral emerging wholeness look like? For without a God of evolution, we have an evolution without God, allowing our dark and blind world to be thrown to the winds of greed and power.

Should we lobby for a God revolution or a revolution of religion? Teilhard's religion of the earth is a radicalization of the core tenets of Christianity. In an unfinished universe where space-time continues to unfold, nothing is complete or fully formed; everything is forming. Everything is open to completion, including the church. This open process of ongoing life is symbolized by the Christ event. Life, death, and resurrection are three dimensions of life's openness to completion in God, and God's future fullness in the whole of life. Everything must die so that everything may live in a new integral (*cosmotheandric*) wholeness. Holmes Rolston writes:

> This whole evolutionary upslope is a calling in which renewed life comes by blasting the old. Life is gathered up in the midst of its throes, a blessed tragedy, lived in grace through a besetting storm. . . . In their lives, beautiful, tragic, and perpetually incomplete, they [all creatures] speak for God; they prophesy as they participate in the divine pathos. . . . They share in the labor of the divinity. . . . The Spirit of God is the genius that makes alive, that redeems life from its evils. The cruciform creation is, in the end, deiform, godly, just because of this element of struggle, not in spite of it. There is a great divine "yes" hidden behind and within every "no" of crushing nature. God, who is the lure toward rationality and sentience . . . is also the compassionate lure in, with, and under all purchasing life the cost of sacrifice. . . . The aura of the cross is cast backward across the whole global story, and it forever outlines the future.[4]

---

[4] Holmes Rolston, III, "Kenosis and Nature," in *The Work of Love,* ed. John Polkinghorne (Grand Rapids, MI: Eerdmans, 2001), 59–60.

The whole evolutionary process is a *via dolorosa* in which suffering, struggle, and death are the wages of a universe in evolution, oriented toward the flourishing of life. Death is the most liberating force of life, and without it we cannot evolve into new levels of complexity-consciousness. However, there are different forms of death. There is the death of brokenness, a type of death that resists the wholeness of life for reasons that are sometimes difficult to comprehend. Such death can be spiritual, emotional, psychological, or physical. Then there is the mystery of death, the untimely death due to accident, violence, or illness, the sudden death that leaves loved ones abandoned without reason or cause. While death comes in many forms, all forms of death are part of the stream of life because every death in some way contributes to the ongoing surge of life.

The type of death Jesus proclaimed was a spiritual death, the death of the isolated self for the sake of greater life. "Those who want to save their life will lose it," he said, "and those who lose their life for the sake of the gospel will save it" (Mk 8:35). Francis of Assisi speaks of death as "sister." "Blessed are those whom death will find in your most holy will," he writes, "for the second death shall do them no harm."[5] He speaks of death not as a radical rupture but as a transformative process, letting go for the sake of new life. I wonder if Pope Francis has reflected on the insight of his namesake. For a church that cannot die, cannot live; and a church that is not alive cannot promote life.

It is time for the church and all world religions to lay down their well-worn pages of doctrine, to consolidate their spiritual paths for a world in evolution, and to yield to a new religion of the earth, one that can gather spiritual energies into a new collective hope. Only if religions work together for the good of the earth can we begin to organically grow

---

[5] Francis of Assisi, "Canticle of the Creatures" in *Francis of Assisi: Early Documents,* vol. 1, *The Saint,* ed. Regis J. Armstrong, J. A. Wayne Hellmann, and William J. Short (New York: New City Press, 1999), 114.

our lives of deep interconnectivity with a vital religious dimension oriented toward the future. How do we go forth? By accepting death as part of life; by holding on to what we cherish, what gives life; and by letting go of the baggage for the sake of greater life. We live in hope that we may move toward the fullness of life.

To resist death is to resist life. The irony is that the denial of death has led to all forms of greed and power, deadly forms of consumption and consumerism that have plundered the planet and alienated the poor. To deny death is to fear life, and we fill the hole of our fears by grasping for things and holding on to them with adamant self-righteousness. Yet the more we hold on with a firm grasp to what is not life, the more quickly we die, for that which we grasp ultimately cannot give us life. Only care for another humanizes us, which is why the death of the isolated self for the sake of greater life requires faith in the power of God. For where there is God, there is love, and where there is love, there is no fear, because the one who lives in love lives freely and celebrates life as belonging to another.

35.

Brother Mango and Eternal Life

*I*t is almost a week since our beloved cat, Mango, was put to sleep. His illness seemed to erupt suddenly. One day he refused to eat, and the next day the same. It was so unlike him, since he was an orange tabby who loved a good dish of tuna. I took him to the vet and was stunned by the news: Mango had abdominal cancer and would last only another week or two. As we watched our beautiful four-legged companion become progressively weaker from lack of nutrition, struggling to get up and down the stairs, a radical life-and-death decision was becoming imminent. On a cold winter afternoon, when the sun was setting in a cloudy sky, we placed Mango in his carrier and tearfully drove to the veterinary clinic. The young woman veterinarian who assisted us was extremely sympathetic to our impending loss and gave us time to say our good-byes to this white-and-orange ball of fur who had stolen our hearts.

We had rescued Mango a little more than eight years earlier, after we began to notice a small white head with two funny ears bobbing up amid the ivy ground cover in the backyard. One day we put a small bowl of milk on the back stoop, and we won his attention. Once inside the house, Mango had found himself a real home. He was not a lap cat but a very faithful one, almost doglike. He did not like men and had a visceral fear of brooms, as if someone had tried to sweep him to death. He answered the door, welcomed people inside by rolling over, and otherwise showed up, like clockwork, for his two square meals and midday snack. He liked to sleep in the chapel and often joined us for prayer in the evening. Mango was real presence. And it is his presence that was sorely missed.

Recent questions in ecology and theology have focused on animal life. Do animals have souls? Do animals go to heaven? Without becoming entangled in theological discourse, I want to say quite clearly that Mango was ensouled. His soul was a core constitutive beingness, a particularity of life that was completely unique, with his own personality and mannerisms. To use the language of Duns Scotus, Mango revealed a *haecceitas,* his own "thisness." Scotus placed a great emphasis on the inherent dignity of each and every thing that exists. We often perceive individual things through their accidental individual characteristics (size, shape, color), but Scotus calls our attention to the "thisness" of each thing, the very being of the object that makes it itself and not something else. *Haecceitas* refers to that positive dimension of every concrete and contingent being that identifies it and makes it worthy of attention, that which can be known only by direct acquaintance and not from consideration of some common nature.

If *haecceitas* is that which is known by direct contact, then *haecceitas* best describes soul. Each living being gives glory to God by its unique, core constitutive being. Soul is what God first utters in every incarnation of the divine Word. Divine love pours itself out in otherness and comes into space-time existence through the life-giving Spirit. To be a creature of God is to be brought into relationship in such a way that the divine mystery is expressed in each concrete existence. Soul is the mirror of creaturely relatedness that reflects the vitality of divine Love.

I did not have to wonder whether or not Mango had a soul. I knew it implicitly by the way he listened to me talking or thinking aloud, the way he sat on my office chair waiting for me to finish writing so he could eat, or simply the way he looked at me—eye to eye—in the early morning, at the start of a new day. Soul existence is expressed in the language of love. I do not think Mango loved me in the same way that I loved him, but his very presence touched my soul in a way that sharing life with Mango enriched my life. Saint Francis of Assisi called all creatures brother and sister. We too called Mango "Brother Mango" and included him as part of our community.

Pierre Teilhard de Chardin realized that the prime energy of the universe is love, a unitive energy that unites center to center, generating more being and life. Love is not a thought or an idea. It is, rather, the transcendent dimension of life itself that reaches out to another, touches the other, and is touched by the other. When we do not share in the fields of love, when we do not feel the concrete existence of another, we can easily abstract the other into a number, a data point, or a joke.

When we recounted Mango's rapid decline to a neighbor, the flippant response was, "Hah! Your first community death!" Without direct contact of core being, without love, a living soul can disappear into the vapors of intellectualism, and we wind up constructing a world of abstract ontology, of lesser beings over greater beings, a ladder of existence in which the human alone stands before God. An intellectualizing of love can lead to hardness of heart, a hardness that can be harder than any rock.

The death of Mango has impelled me to reflect on what matters most in life, what breaks the human heart and what nurtures the deep, relational dimension of all life. Saint Paul writes, "If I have prophetic powers, and understand all mysteries and all knowledge, and if I have all faith, so as to remove mountains, but do not have love, I am nothing" (1 Cor 13:3).

Love makes us *something*; it makes us alive and draws us in to the dynamism of life, sustaining life's flow despite many layers of sufferings and disappointments. The person who cannot love cannot suffer, for that person is without grief, without feeling, and indifferent. If God is love, then the vitality of love, even the love of a furry creature, *is* the dynamic presence of God.

Hans Urs von Balthasar writes of the vulnerability of God's love: "It is God's going forth into the danger and the nothingness of the creation that reveals his heart to be at its origin vulnerable."[1] Out of the fullness of God's self-giving love, God shares in the pain and suffering of the world. God bends low to share our tears out of a heart full of mercy and love—and we are caught up in the divine embrace.

Divine love bending low is what gives the *haecceitas* of every creature a mark of eternal endurance. Every creature is born out of the love of God, sustained in love, and transformed in love. Every sparrow that falls to the ground is known and loved by God (cf. Mt 10:29); the Spirit of God is present in love to each creature here and now so that all creaturely life shares in cosmic communion. Bonaventure says that Christ has something in common with all creatures and all things are transformed in Christ. Heaven is where all tears and sufferings are wiped away, where each life is opened to the unlimited, divine, creative love and a cosmic communion of all created life is realized in the fullness of Christ.

As I reflect on Mango's death, his *haecceitas*, and the mystery of love, I have no doubt that his core love-energy will endure. His life has been inscribed on mine; the memory of his life is entangled with my own. My heart grieves for Brother Mango, my faithful companion, but I believe we shall be reunited in God's eternal embrace.

---

[1] Hans Urs von Balthasar, *The Glory of the Lord: A Theological Aesthetics*, trans. Andrew Louth, Francis McDonagh, and Brian McNeil, vol. 2, *Studies in Theological Style: Clerical Styles* (San Francisco: Ignatius Press, 1984), 356.

Conclusion

A single human life is like the expanse of the whole universe. It erupts in time and develops through pain and struggle into freedom of identity. Strange is this process of life filled with joy and tears, a lifelong journey through narrow tunnels and dark passages into an infinite horizon of life that transcends the human mind, the infinite freedom of life itself. The psalmist writes:

> The days of our life are seventy years
> or perhaps eighty, if we are strong;
> even then their span is only toil and trouble;
> they are soon gone, and we fly away. (Ps 90:10)

It is mysterious that a human struggles through each day to become someone, only to die. In a 13.8–billion-year-old universe filled with billions of galaxies and stars, such struggle to attain a cosmic moment of identity is either completely ludicrous or infinitely precious. We have no way to judge the worth of a single human life except against the background of life itself, revealed in scripture as "I Am," *Yahweh-Yireh,* or simply, God. And we have no way to know anything about this ultimate source of life except that its ultimacy is what drives us to continue on through life's challenges. Every single human life is a question about God, a question answered by the engagement of life itself.

The human person is the conscious mind of the universe, created to know and to love; the whole universe is oriented to knowledge and love, from the smallest particles of life to the inventors of tomorrow. What we know and how we know shapes what we love and how we love. All knowledge is ultimately beholden to love. Our greatest striving is for unity and transcendence, whether it is solving a computer problem, finding a vaccine, writing a poem, or playing with the kids on a Saturday afternoon. If love is the reason we exist, then relationality is our deepest reality. We belong to one another because we belong to an infinite heart of love. God is love and continues to love the world into a unity of mind and heart. Heaven is where God's life and our life become so intertwined that divine and created life are dynamically entangled in everlasting love. But we are far from this ultimate reality as a collective whole and thus the universe will continue on for billions of years. I think far into the future a new species with a new God consciousness will emerge, a species that will be at home with other species of cosmic intelligent life, attaining a level of divinely centered intergalactic consciousness that exceeds anything we can ask or imagine; an intergalactic consciousness steeped in love. This will be the second coming of Christ.

So what should we do in our present moment? The essays in this book have tried to convey meaning and direction to allay the challenges we face. We must wake up from the deep slumber of our isolated egocentric lives and become attuned to the universe that is our home. The new universe story is the intercommunion of life itself, of each part with the whole. Everything is in communion in the vast web of the universe. The intense communion within the material world enables life to emerge into being. Living forms are differentiated, and subjectivity emerges as a result of communion within itself and with the environment. The connector of life, what holds all the different levels of communion together, is consciousness, and consciousness is driven by love, that is, the power of attraction.

Pierre Teilhard de Chardin saw a center of personal communion at the heart of existence itself; this center is the living God who is within each aspect of material existence and ahead of everything that exists. God is relationship, a Trinity of love. All that exists is born out of relationship, exists in relationship, and is oriented toward eternal relationship in love. Anything and everything that disrupts, thwarts, stifles, or destroys the relationality of a single life, destroys the living God.

I have tried to point out gently that we have been eradicating the living God for (at least) the last century, and unless we begin to find the living God once again by stepping outside the boxes we have placed God into and returning to the first book of revelation, the "Book of Nature," we are destined to face catastrophes. Francis of Assisi found God in the cathedral of the universe. For Francis, nature was a place of prayer, worship, and community and spiritual transformation; in this church of life he learned to live in the widest embrace of love. We too must learn from nature how to be part of nature once again, so that we can join with nature in the evolution of love. For how we live is how we die, and how we die through the daily sacrifices of deepening love is how we will live forever.

No life is inconsequential; every life has ultimate value. We do not have power over anyone's life except our own, and even this power is limited by our ability to choose. Every life affects every other life because from the beginning of time we have belonged to another. The best of religion is centered on this reality. To have faith is to believe in the other who we are related to on the fundamental level of life. Without a consciousness of interrelatedness, we are entrapped in the illusion of separateness. Religion has done a disservice by making God an object of our attention rather than the ground of our lives, as if God might actually be a person distinct from us. Today we must rediscover God in order to be at home in the universe with one another and the wider world of nature.

There is no easy or sure path to God and the fullness of
life. The whole of life is a trial-and-error experiment and the
only thing we can do well is to remain faithful. For God is
faithful and will not fail us, even if we blindly destroy our
planet. God mourns the profound loss of life we inflict on
the planet, but remains ever faithful in love. God is love, and
we are continuously invited to rise up from the deadness of
our lives and love anew. For where God is, there is infinite
mercy; God's divine heart is always ready to forgive, forget,
and embrace. God is the name of absolute hope and future.

To reflect on a day of life in the universe is to recognize
that death is our greatest reality for, in truth, the end is in the
present moment. In this moment we must make every effort
to love. In this moment the whole universe awaits the final
reason for my life, summed up in one question that each of
us must constantly live into: How well did I love this day?
For in the evening of life, love alone will determine how we
shall live forever.

Index

Page numbers in italics refer to poetic interludes.

9/11, xi

Abrams, Nancy Ellen, 61
absolute power, 74
"Agony of Our Age, The"
    (Teilhard), 219
Al-Khalili, Jim, 7
animal life, 235–36
Anselm, Saint, 228
anthropology, theological 95.
    See also personhood
anxiety, 205
apatheia, 164
apocalypse, 172
Apple, 179–80
Appletopia (Robinson), 179
Aquinas. *See* Thomas Aquinas
Aristarchus, 181
Aristotle, 7, 88–89, 181
Arius, 108
artificial intelligence, 81, 136
Athanasius, 108
Atmanspacher, Harald, 23
Augustine, Saint, 103, 127,
    193
Auribondo, Sri, 93
Axial Age (Jaspers), 116–119
axial consciousness, 115,
    116–17; and religion,
    119–20

Balthasar, Hans Urs von, 238
baptism, 10
Barbour, Ian, 95
Barnhart, Bruno, OSB Cam.,
    165
beauty, 70, 72–73
Being (Heidegger), 29
Benedict XVI, Pope, 93
Bergson, Henri, 16, 211–12
Bernard of Clairvaux, 128
Berry, Thomas, CP, 83, 190,
    225
Big Bang theory, 80
biodiversity loss, 57, 77
Birth of a Dancing Star (De-
    lio), 48–49
black holes, 4
Black, Anthony, 119
Body of Christ, 173–74
Bohm, David, 23, 137, 149
Bonaventure, Saint, 13
    on Christ, 28, 31, 36, 74–
    75, 105
    on contemplation, 162
    on creation, 59, 60, 69–70,
    74, 88
    on knowledge, 172
    on love, 128, 207
Bourgeault, Cynthia, 31–32
Brague, Remi, 39–40
Bruteau, Beatrice, 93–95, 96–
    99, 113, 121, 133, 166
Buddhism, 105, 199, 224

"Canticle of Creatures" (Francis of Assisi), 59–60, 194, 195
"Canticle of the Feathered Ones" (Thomsen), 171
capax infiniti, 206
Capture (Kessler), 131
Carson, Rachel, 189
Carter, J. Kameron, 120
centeredness, 42, 151
Chalcedon, Council of (425), 109, 201
chaos, 9–11, 138
charity, 183
Christ Omega, 64
"Christic, The" (Teilhard), 66
Christogenesis, 43, 64
Christology, 45–46, 50, 107–10, 201; cosmic, 13–14, 56, 103–4, 139, 194
Christophany (Panikkar), 48, 109
church, 56, 66, 90, 140–41, 194, 233
Ciszek, Walter, SJ, 132
civil disobedience, 165
Clare of Assisi, Saint, 192
Classics of Western Spirituality series (Paulist), 163
clericalism, 120
co-creation. *See* humanity, as co-creators
communion, 152, 240
community, 169, 194, 212
complexification, xiii, 22, 228
compression, human, 219
consciousness, 9–10, 21, 23, 29, 81, 96, 151, 200, 240
  and divinity, 24
  types of, 98–99

collective, 15, 192
evolutionary, 159
global, xiii, 65, 122, 152
neo-feminine (Bruteau), 98
social, 165
unitive, 156
consumerism, 45, 81, 117, 144, 183, 186–87, 190
contemplation, 157–59, 160–62, 163–67, 214–15
  and action, 165, 167
contemplative energetic (Laird), 161, 166, 214
convergence, xiv, 64–65, 94, 191, 223
conversion, xii
Copernicus, Nicholas, 60, 181
cosmic Christ. *See* Christology, cosmic
cosmic personalization (Teilhard), 16–17
cosmogenesis, 211
cosmologization (Brague), 39–40
cosmology, 1–2, 211
  medieval, 60, 88
cosmotheandricity, xv, , 45–47, 155, 174, 232
Cousins, Ewert, 163
COVID-19, xi, 143–45, 169, 171, 172, 189, 194, 227
creation, 51–52, 59, 70
  and incarnation, 74
creativity, 51, 72, 200–201
cross, 36–37, 195, 207
Crucified God, The (Moltmann), 36–37
cybernetics, 90, 139–40, 180, 189
cyberspace, 89–90, 189

cyborg. *See* cybernetics
Cyril of Alexandria, 108
Darwin, Charles, xiii, 181
death of God. *See* God, death of (Nietzsche)
death, 5, 85, 172, 174, 187, 207, *217–18*, 227, 233, 235, 242
deep ecology, 79
deforestation, 77, 84
detachment, 224
digital natives, 223
Dirac, Paul, 30
discernment, 8, 9
discipleship, 163, 164, 167
disenchantment, 206
dispossession. *See* poverty, voluntary
Divine Milieu, The (Teilhard), 82, 213–14
divinization, 166
docetism, 56
dual-aspect monism, 21, 22–23
dualism, metaphysical, 119
Duns Scotus. *See* John Duns Scotus
Dyophysitism, 109
Dyson, Freeman, 57, 77

Easter Triduum, 194, 196
Eckhart, Meister, 10, 25, 48, 158
ecological crisis. *See* environmental crisis
Einstein, Albert, 3, 5, 137, 181
élan vital (Bergson), 211
emergence, 22
empirical method, 14–15
energy, 23, 159, 211

Enlightenment, 120
environmental crisis, 57, 77–78, 87. *See also* biodiversity loss; global warming; water scarcity
eternity, *19–20*
ethics, 40, 43
Eucharist, 10, 173–74, 185, 192–93
Evagrius Ponticus, 164
evolution, xii–xiii, 13–14, 16, 61, 67, 94–100, *147*, 181, 205, 228
  and education, 223
  and religion, xii, 222–23, 229–30
  biological, 22, 138–39
  creative, 16
  human, 24, 80, 220–22
  of sex, 111–12
experience, 22

faith, 31, 133, 151, 161, 241
fear, 35
forgiveness, 133, *197–98*, 202, 208–9
fractals, 138
fragility, 35
Francis of Assisi, Saint
  on creation, 59–60, 69, 87, 184–86, 194, 195, 241
  on Christ, 69, 185
  on death, 233
  and the Eucharist, 192
  and love, 75
  and prayer, 155
  and poverty, voluntary, 185–86, 224
Francis, Pope
  on creation, 59, 73–75

on environmental crisis, 57–58, 61, 92
on evolution, 62–63, 66, 75
and Francis of Assisi, 69, 233
on love, 59
on science, 140
See also Laudato Si' (Pope Francis)
freedom, 70, 71–72, 129
fundamental theology, 139

Gates, Bill, 143
Gaudium et spes (Vatican II), 163
gender, 112–13
   fluidity, 121
   polarization, 111
geomnesia, 190
Gilson, Étienne, 13
global warming, 57, 58, 84, 85, 87, 135, 172, 177, 214
globalization, 223
Gnosticism, 56
God, 6, 9–11, *19–20*, 24–26, 63, 100, 127, 239
   birth of, 24–25
   death of (Nietzsche), 120
   and evolution, 41–42
   as gift, 184
   knowledge of, 114
   as love, 103–4, 141, 175, 228, 240, 242
   Omega, 129–30, 151, 157, 166, 213–15
   reign of, xi, 107
   as Trinity, 105, 241
   and world, xvi, 24–25, 41, 231

See also suffering, divine; love, divine; grace, divine; will, divine
God without Being (Marion), 184
Goff, Phillip, 21–22
Golding, William, 173
Good Samaritan, parable of the, 27
goodness, 127, 144, 152
Gore, Al, 14, 78
grace, divine, 41, 50
gratitude, 184–85
gravitational waves, 3–6
Great Chain of Being, 88
Greek fathers, 13
Greene, Brian, 227, 230
Gregory of Nyssa, 164
Grosseteste, Robert, 3
Guardini, Romano, 93

haeccitas (John Duns Scotus). *See* thisness
Hafiz, 114
Harari, Yuval, 178–79
He Leadeth Me (Ciszek), 132
heaven, 240
Hegel, 139
Heidegger, Martin, 29, 139
heliocentrism, 60, 80
hell, 35
Heraclitus, 224
Hidden Life of Trees, The (Wohlleben), 149
Hillesum, Etty, 33, 186
Hinduism, Advaitic, 24, 45
"Historical Roots of Our Ecologic Crisis" (White), 57, 90
Homo Deus (Harari), 178

Homo sapiens, 115
Hooper, Daniel, 112
Hopkins, Gerard Manley, 88, 157
"How I Believe" (Teilhard), 15
Hugh of St. Victor, 28
humanity, autonomy of, 116
   dominion over nature, 57
   as co-creators, xiv, 65, 113
Human Metaphor, The (Sewell), 15
Humani generis (Pope Pius XII), 62–63, 75, 95
humility, divine, 36
Huxley, Julian, 24, 81
hybridization, 201
"Hymn to Matter" (Teilhard), 162
hyperpersonal (Teilhard), 191

identity, 116
imago Dei, 119
immanence, divine, 84
immutability, divine, 43
impermanence, 224
incarnation, 24, 28, 46, 55, 119
   and creation, 74
individualism, 120
   religious, 15
Ingham, Mary Beth, CSJ, 72
interconnectedness, 58, 69, 96, 116, 140, 200, 230–31, 234. *See also* relationality
interiority, 42, 151
internet, 189–90, 205
internet religion, 193
interrelatedness. *See* relationality

interspirituality, 121
Irenaeus of Lyons, 103
Islam, 105

Jaspers, Karl, 116, 118
Jesus Christ, *101–2*, 107–10, *147, 198*
   body of, 196
   and cosmos, 65
   descent into hell, 35
   divinity of, 108
   as event, 232
   as gift, 185
   humanity of, 109
   and love, 104–5, 238
   nativity of, 29, 183–84, 185
   oneness with God, 9
   presence in others, 28
   teachings of, 85, 140, 174–75, 202, 238
   See also Christ Omega; Christogenesis; Christology; Christophany (Panikkar)
Jobs, Steve, 143, 167, 180
John Duns Scotus, 59, 70–73, 103–4, 236
John of the Cross, Saint, 130
John Paul II, Saint, 93
John, Elton, 111
Judaism, 105, 169
Julian of Norwich, 178
Jung, Carl, 23
justice, 153, 165

Kant, Immanuel, 40, 139
Kessler, David A., 131
King, Thomas, SJ, 54
Knitter, Paul, 47n10
knowledge, 240

Krebs cycle, 200
Kuhn, Thomas, 181

Laird, Martin, 160–61, 166, 214
Laser Interferometer Gravitational-Wave Observatory (LIGO), 4
Lateran IV Council, 192
Laudato Si' (Pope Francis), 57, 59, 61–63, 65, 66–67, 69, 73–75, 93–95, 177
Lent, 201–2
LGBTQ community, 113
Life on the Edge (McFadden and Al-Khalili), 7–8
light, 3, 228
lila (Hinduism), 199
liturgy. *See* worship
Lomax, Eric, 207–8
Lord of the Flies (Golding), 173
Lorenz, Edward, 138
Lossky, Vladimir, 33
love, 9, 16, 32, *51–52*, 66, 73, 122–23, 127–30, 145, 173, *197–98*, 237, 240–41
  chaotic, 11
  costly, 208–9
  divine, 28–31, 37–38, 49, 53, 59, 70–72, 105–6, 158, 195, 228
  and forgiveness, 133
  four stages of (Bernard), 128
  perfection of, 73
Luce, De (Grosseteste), 3

Malone, Patrick, SJ, 31
Marion, Jean-Luc, 184

Marrotti, Paola, 212
materiality, 53–56, 70, 151, 157
McFadden, Johnjoe, 7
McGilchrist, Ian, 116
McKibben, Bill, 79–80
memory, 131
mercy, 32
  divine, 33–34
Merton, Thomas, OCSO, 110, 158, 213
Minkowski, Herbert, 137
modernity, 40, 88–89, 189, 206
Moltmann, Jürgen, 36–37
monasticism, 160
monism/panpsychism, 21–22
Monophysitism, 109
Moore, Gordon, 90, 205, 221–22
morality, emergence of, 118
mycelium, 150
mystery, 5–6, *19–20*, 25
mysticism, 54
myth, 115

Naess, Arne, 79
Nagase, 208
narcissism, 205
natural law, 43
natural philosophy/science, 13
natural selection, 8, 14
nature
  dynamism of, 199–200, 211, 221
  stability of, 212
Neanderthals, 115
new creation, 11
New Universe and the Human Future, The (Abrams and Primack), 61

Newton, Isaac, Sir, 7, 89, 181
Newtonian physics, 3, 58
Nicholas of Cusa, 60
Nietzsche, Friedrich, 120
noosphere (Teilhard), 65

observation, 3
Olson, Ed, 8
Omega principle (Teilhard), 16, 212, 228. *See also* God; Omega
Origen, 103, 164
original sin, 64, 103, 190

panentheism, 55, 74
Panikkar, Raimon, xv, 25, 45–48, 50, 63, 109, 178
Pannenberg, Wolfhart, 159
panpsychism, 21, 228,
pantheism, 55
passibility, divine. *See* suffering, divine
patriarchy, 119
Paul, Saint, 13, 56, 237
Pauli, Wolfgang, 22
Paulist Press, 163
Pearly Gates of Cyberspace (Wertheim), 88
perception, 14
perfection, divine, 42
personhood, xii, 97–98, 113–14, 120, 169
  beauty of, 169
  as performative, 122
  transcendent, 99
Phenomenon of Man, The (Teilhard), 14
physics, 21–22
Pius XII, Pope, 62–63, 75, 95
Plato, 163
Plotinus, 163–64, 214

pluralism, 139
"Position of Man in Nature and the Significance of Human Socialization, The" (Teilhard), 23–24
posthuman, 121
poverty, voluntary, 185–86, 187, 224
power, divine, 108
prayer, 54, 131, 155, 157, 158–59, 231–32
pre-axial consciousness, 115–16
Prensky, Marc, 223
presence, divine, xvii, 14, 55–56, 70, 108, 237
Primack, Joel, 61
Primum Mobile, 88
providence, divine, 132
Pseudo-Dionysius, 35

quantum physics, 7, 8, 15, 22, 23, 96, 137, 200

race, 115, 116, 120
Rahner, Karl, SJ, 139
Railway Man, The (film), 207–8
rationality, 73, 118
Rees, William, 78
reign of God. *See* God, reign of
relationality, *51–52*
  of cosmos, 59, 96
  deep, 119, 200, 231
  divine, 42–43, 49, 85
  of humanity, 59, 96, 98
  Pope Francis on 59, 67
  of life, 79, 85, 96, 199–202
  and love, 127, 129, 143–45
  new types of, 120

relativity, 180
  general, 3
  special, 137
religion, 65–66, 79, 119, 169, 241
  of the earth, 65–66, 84, 152, 169
  and science, 61, 150
religiosity, 5
ressourcement, 163
resurrection, 174, 203, 208
revelation, 160
Rhythm of Being, The (Panikkar), xv
Rilke, Rainer Maria, 92
ritual, 116
Robinson, Brett, 179–80
Rocketman (film), 111
Rohr, Richard, OFM, 103–4
Rolheiser, Ronald, OMI, 112
Rolston, Holmes, III, 228, 232
Rupert of Deutz, 103

sacramentality, 70
Sagan, Carl, 57, 77
salvation, 103
"Salvation by Algorithm" (Harari), 178
sanctification, 42
Sapiens (Harari), 178
Scholasticism, xv–xvi, 16, 69
Schrödinger, Erwin, 8–9
"Scientific Research as Adoration" (King), 54
Scotus. *See* John Duns Scotus
scripture, 13
second axial consciousness, 120, 230
Sewell, Elizabeth, 15
sex, as disconnection, 112
sexuality, 111, 113

Silent Spring (Carson), 189
Simard, Suzanne, 150
sin, 64, 103
social distancing, 189
social justice. *See* justice
social media, 56
soul, 63, 236
Soul's Journey into God (Bonaventure), 36
space exploration, 81
space-time, 3, 5
Spirit, *125–26*
"Spiritual Power of Matter, The" (Teilhard), 53–54, 155–56
spirituality, Franciscan, 162
spondic energy (Bruteau), 97
Stein, Edith, 29–30
suffering, xi, 32, 53, 92, 106, 156, *197*, 207, 233
  divine, 36–37, 195

Teilhard de Chardin, Pierre, SJ, xiii–xvi, 41–43, 53–56, 173, 227
  anthropology of, 23–24, 61, 63, 211–14
  and contemplation, 155–57, 159–62, 166, 213–14
  cosmology of, 23–24, 61, 81–82
  death of, 17
  and evolution, xiv, 94–95, 219–21, 228, 231
  on love, 104, 128–29, 200, 207, 237
  and religion, 65–67, 81, 91, 150–52, 192, 193, 229
  on technology, 64–65, 191
  theology of, 13–14, 53–56, 64, 104, 231, 241

See also cosmic personalization (Teilhard); hyperpersonal (Teilhard); noosphere (Teilhard); Omega principle (Teilhard)
technology, xiv, 65, 78, 81, 90–92, 143, 189–90, 230
   advent of, 120
   effects on humanity, 90–91, 180, 205–6
   and evolution, 221
   and nature, 136
   as religion, 39, 135–36, 179–80, 190
   speed of, 39, 90, 205, 221–22
Teresa of Avila, Saint, 178
theodicy, 36
thisness, 104, 158, 236, 238
Thomas Aquinas, Saint, xv, 69, 88, 162, 230
Thomas of Celano, 155, 185
Thompson, William M., 117
Thompson-Uberuaga, William. *See* Thompson, William M.
Thomsen Sara, 171
Thorne, Kip, 4
Thunberg, Greta, 135, 177
transcendence, 200–201
"Trinitarian Personhood" (Bruteau), 97
Turing, Alan, 143

übermensch (Nietzsche), 120
ultrahumanism, 43, 214, 215
Universal Christ, The (Rohr), 103
Until the End of Time (Greene), 227
urban life, 118

Vacek, Edward, SJ, 42
Vatican II Council, xv, 163
violence, 227
vision, 167

water scarcity, 57
wave-particle duality, 7
wealth, 144
Weber, Max, 144
Wertheim, Margaret, 88–89
White, Lynn, Jr., 57, 78, 81, 87, 90, 91
Whitehead, Alfred North, 24, 80, 137
will,
   divine, 42, 71–72, 132
   human, 73
With God in Russia (Ciszek), 132
Wohlleben, Peter, 149
worship, 54, 192–93

zimzum (divine withdrawal), 61

CPSIA information can be obtained
at www.ICGtesting.com
Printed in the USA
LVHW081316250521
688446LV00019B/622

9 781626 984035